ETHNIC IDENTITY AND NATIONAL LOYALTY OF AN ETHNIC GROUP

By The Same Author

1. Building Skill and Capability Among Gram Panchayat *(In press)*
2. Capacity Building for Local Body Leaders
3. Dynamics of New Panchayati Raj System in India (in 15 volumes series)
4. Emerging Dimensions in Decentralisation *(In press)*
5. Functional Efficiency of Gram Sabha in Tamil Nadu *(In press)*
6. Grassroot Democracy in Indian Society
7. New Panchayati Raj System at Work : An Evaluation
8. New Panchayati Raj in Tamil Nadu (with Act in Original)
9. Process and Performance of Gram Panchayat Women and Dalit Presidents (with 38 case studies of Tamil Nadu Panchayats) *(In press)*
10. Rural Transformation and People's Entitlement's

About the Author

Ganapathi Palanithurai, Dean, Faculty of Social Sciences; Member Syndicate, Coordinator in Rajiv Gandhi Chair; Gandhigram Rural Institute; and Head, Department of Political Science and Development Administration, Gandhigram Rural University, Tamil Nadu, is an academic activist working with the people in rural areas to reinvent sustainable grassroots democracy. He is also associated in different capacities with the Planning Commission of India, State Planning Commission of Tamil Nadu, Population Foundation of India, Ford Foundation, UNICEF, Rajiv Gandhi Foundation, CAPART, Ministry of Rural Areas and Employment, and DANIDA.

Prof. Palanithurai has to his credit thirty-two books, seventy-nine articles, twelve working papers, seven monographs and seven review articles. He was a recipient of fellowship from Sastri Indo-Canadian Institute, New Delhi, and World Academy of Art and Science, USA. Also, he is a member of the Expert Committee, constituted by the Government of Tamil Nadu to monitor the training programme for local body leaders. He is Chairperson of the Hunger Project Council in Tamil Nadu as well.

ETIINIC IDENTITY AND NATIONAL LOYALTY OF AN ETHNIC GROUP

A Case Study of Tamil Nadu

G. PALANITHURAI

Department of Political Science and Development Administration

Gandhigram Rural Institute — Deemed University

Gandhigram-624302

CONCEPT PUBLISHING COMPANY, NEW DELHI-110059

Cataloging in Publication Data—DK
Courtesy: D.K. Agencies (P) Ltd. <docinfo@dkagencies.com>

Palanithurai, G. (Ganapathy), 1953-
Ethnic identity and national loyalty of an ethnic group : a case study of Tamil Nadu / G. Palanithurai.
p. cm.
Includes bibliographical references (p.)
Includes index.
ISBN 8180691446

1. Ethnicity—Political aspects—India—Tamil Nadu. 2. Nationalism—India—Tamil Nadu—History. I. Title.

DDC 305.800 954 82 21

ISBN 81-8069-144-6

First Published, 2005

Published and Printed by
Ashok Kumar Mittal
Concept Publishing Company
A/15-16, Commercial Block, Mohan Garden,
New Delhi-110059 (INDIA)

Phones : 25351460, 25351794
Fax : 091-11-25357103
E-mail : publishing@conceptpub.com

To

The Divine Mother

PREFACE

Nation-States, through governments, promised benefits and services to the people of different collectivities by taking away many of the responsibilities of communities. The Government's growth in terms of structure and functions has pushed the people away from the orbit of governance and made them onlookers and beneficiaries of the government. As a result the people have started looking at the government from the point of view of benefits. People are now being organized as groups with an identity with the objective of getting legitimate benefits from the government. Groups have developed a variety of devices to project their demands and to get their problems solved. To bring about cohesiveness among the people the leaders of groups adopt different nuances. The process of interaction between the government and groups is in a continuum. This phenomenon prevails in almost all the societies of the world barring a few. In India there are a variety of ethnic groups, of which the Dravidian Movement is a significant one.

The Dravidian Movement gained momentum as an ethnic movement in the Indian political system. People had been oriented and consceintized for about five decades on ethnic values and, as a result, political parties emerged from the same ethnic movement to realise the basic objectives of the movement. Over a period of time the course of the movement has changed.

Once the formation of group identity was seriously visualized by scholars and projected as detrimental to the unity of the Nation-State. Later this kind of visualization changed and the formation of ethnic identity was recognized as a factor for the development of a group or community. In Tamil Nadu when ethnic identity was projected it was constructed as an anti-national activity but now the ethnic political parties have joined hands with the national political parties to participate in the process of the Indian political system by which the initial doubts were cleared.

This study focuses its attention on the linkage between ethnic identity and national loyalty. It further analyses the nature of the relationship between ethnic identity and national loyalty. It dispels many of the doubts regarding the linkages. It throws new light on the interface between the two, to the effect that the stronger ethnic identity is in no way detrimental to national loyalty and in fact a strong ethnic identity reinforces national loyalty. By conducting a field study in two districts, namely Ramanathapuram and Coimbatore, the main hypotheses deduced from the theory on ethnicity has been tested. This study highlights the paradoxical situations contextually in the ethnic politics of Tamil Nadu.

Gandhigram **G. Palanithurai**

ACKNOWLEDGEMENTS

The idea of this study struck my mind when I was in Montreal of Quebec Province to study the problems of the 'Party Quebecois' in Canada. I was reading an article written by an activist of the 'Party Quebecois' about his position as a separatist. He argued that he was always keeping two identities, but only one identity was projected by the federal government and the other was not seen by the same government, which branded him an ethnic leader. His contributions to Canada were not highlighted but his activities for the ethnic movement were blown up beyond proportion. I was reminded of a speech of Mr. M. Karunanidhi the president of the DMK party in Tamil Nadu. In his speech he quoted how he and his party stood with the nation to maintain unity and integrity during all turbulent periods. Hence I decided to undertake a study to test dual identity or multiplicity of identity and its implications in the ethnic movement, especially in the case of the Dravidian Movement from the perspective of the members of an ethnic movement. I have carried out this work with the financial support of ICSSR, New Delhi. I would like to place on record my sincere thanks to ICSSR for its financial assistance to carry out this work. Further I must thank the respondents for their patience in responding to my questions and for sparing their valuable time for me. For the completion of any work successfully the environmental condition prevailing in the work place is more important than any other factors and, in this regard, the atmosphere at Gandhigram Rural Institute is always congenial for creative work, for which I must thank the founders of the Institute Dr. Soundaram and Dr. G. Ramachandran for their noble ideas and the successive authorities of the Institute for their effective leadership.

Four persons worked with me on this endeavour: Mr. K. Tamilarasan in collecting data from the field; Mr. S.P. Ramesh computed the data; Dr. M.A. Jeyaraju read my manuscript; and Mr. G. Rajan typed the document. I profusely thank all the four, particularly Dr. M.A. Jeyaraju for vetting my manuscript with a sense of commitment. My colleagues in the department and in the projects helped me immensely to carry out my work without any hindrance. I thank them for their co-operation and kindness towards me. Equally my family, more particularly my affectionate wife Mrs. Mala, relieved me from the family burden to devote my attention wholly to academic assignments. Hence I express my deep sense of appreciation and gratitude to my wife Mrs. Mala and my beloved children Senthil and Aurobindh.

G. PALANITHURAI

CONTENTS

1

INTRODUCTION

Ethnicity is a subject of study in the recent years in many disciplines of social. This concept has gained momentum in the academic world as the socio-political processes have been moving in a direction which is quite opposite to the expectations of the liberals and socialists over one and a half century despite the development of the Nation-State system and mass communication. Human beings are decisively in search of an identity to form a group to exert pressure on the government to maximise the allocation, both in terms of decisions and resources for their advantage. Materially developed nations would not witness such conflict as per the perception of the scholars in the initial stage of theory building on ethnicity. But the reality is shocking: ethnic conflict has assumed such proportion of intensity in taking away lives even in the economically affluent countries[1]. Million have lost their lives in ethnic and racial conflincts[2]. When this conflict syndrome was witnessed in the 1950s in the developing nations, it was believed that it was a third world phenomenon which could be controlled, regulated and managed by following westernization, modernization and developing mass communication. Prescriptions have been offered from the American universities through their reports to the societies of the third world. Their eyes were opened only in the 60s and 70s when a number of ethnic conflicts erupted in North American and European countries[3].

Academics wondered about the new puzzle and started looking into the genesis of this problem and tried to bring our general propositions about ethnic identities[4], conflicts[5] and conflict management[6]. Systematic studies have been conducted[7], institutions have been developed[8], scholars from different disciplines have been drawn, funds have been mobilised to investigate the problem across the borders of countries and Nation-States[9]. Theories, theoretical frameworks and methodological nuances have been developed over the years and yet the depth of the problem could not be studied. Ethnicity has assumed such significance that ministries are formed, political recruitments are made, administrative staff selections are made, and even recruitment of personnel for army is made on ethnic considerations, because ethnicity is a core and central issue in the socio-political life of the people in the world today.

From the beginning of the academic exercise on ethnicity, scholars have been developing perspectives to look at ethnic issues from an alarmist perspective as if ethnic groups are always detrimental to the consolidation of the Nation-State and will always work against the integration of the nation[10]. The scholars' consideration was the primacy of the Nation-State the instrument of development and social justice[11]. While analysing the whole gamut of ethnic group activities in the past three or four decades scholars cannot establish that ethnic group activities always lead to disintegration of the nation. At the same time they cannot advance the proposition that ethnic groups will not lead to autonomy or total independence from the state system. The process has variations in terms of formation of group identity[12], activating groups for political tasks[13], leadership qualities[14], bargaining capacity of leaders[15], capacity of the states, conflict management formula[16], assimilation of the ethnic groups[17] in the mainstream and declaring independence from the state. There are instances in the world of ethnic groups who have gone to the level of demanding total independence from the Nation-State and then have receded and been assimilated in the mainstream. Likewise there are groups which have posited only ethnic demands and gradually moved to declaration of independence and won their independence also. There are Nation-States which have evolved management formulas to resolve ethnic conflicts to the satisfaction of ethnic groups by solving their problems and there are another set of Nation-States which are always suppressive in character and have suppressed ethnic groups through authoritarian decisions. One can see varieties of ethnicity in the world.

Human beings are grouped for specific functions. The groupings have several logistics from the perspective of the members of the groups and that of others who look at the groups as outsiders. Members need not necessarily be members of the same group for ever as their membership is not a bond binding them inseparably with a group. The basic question is why an individual identifies himself or herself with an organisation. The reasons are many. Economic benefit, self-esteem, community satisfaction, family satisfaction are some of the reasons. Individuals affiliate themselves to several organisations simultaneously. The intensity of their affiliation depends on their perception of the profit, they gain from the organisation. The profit need not necessarily be material in nature. It may take any form. The boundary of any group varies from time-to-time. The activities of the groups will affect the functioning of legitimate institutions from the regional level to the international level.

An individual's consciousness of himself or herself in terms of his or her nation, region, religion, language, culture, clan, tribe and so on is a continuous process. The intensity of the consciousness will vary from period to period. In one particular context the intensity of an individual in affiliating himself or herself to an organisation may be very high or low. But all these activities of the individuals and groups are being visualised from the perspective of the legitimate governing institutions. In the contemporary world the human socio-political activities are looked at from a variety of perspective like nation building, or national integration, or state formation and so on. The very basis of this approach is that the Nation-State is an imperative need of human development and peace and hence any activity which is against the Nation-State is considered harmful to humanity. Contrary to this belief system, there are issues in society which are not considered by Nation-State through its instrument of government. All these vital issues are projected to the legitimate authorities unless the social and economic disparities can be eliminated from the existing arrangement. The individuals with different identities are motivated and mobilised to project their demands to the authorities of the state for decision-making. In the process of mobilising the people under one banner or the other issues are highlighted and the state authorities are alerted and given an opportunity to tackle them and they are tackled. Thus it is dynamic process visualised from the perspective of the people.

At present group activities are seen as vibrant or vital in the political process of modern governments and this is being visualised from the backdrop of a new concept – ethnicity. Ethnicity is not a new phenomenon. It is as old as human civilization itself. It is new only in terms of nomenclature and approach[18]. The roots of ethnicity are in culture, language, caste etc., which are all inherent and in-built in human civilization. This problem was not seriously considered for many years. But suddenly, it picked up momentum among academics as it claimed the life of several million people in the world in the name of religion, race, culture and language. Theories, theoretical frameworks, models, new concepts, new tools of analysis have been developed by academics of different disciplines of social science from Anthropology to Political Science over the years. In the process of analysing the dynamics of the relationship between groups and the state, academics has started emphasising the importance of humanity and they are now oriented to analyse the issues from the perspective of the people rather than from the perspective of the state. Institutions have been started to study this phenomenon. Over the last three decades voluminous works has been carried out in Cultural Anthropology, Sociology, Psychology, Political Science and Economics. Yet the understanding of the issues is not quite clear as the issues are culture-bound, region-bound and contextual.

In a democratic polity expressing grievances to the state authorities is an accepted principle in the democratic process of decision-making. Why should the State take an alarmist perspective of the articulations of grievances by the people through an organised group against the backdrop of a particular identity? This has been seriously viewed mainly in the new nations, since, being new to democratic governance, many of them have gone to an authoritarian form of government.

More specifically in the Asian region, countries which were liberated from the yoke of the British in the middle of the 20th century began to follow the parliamentary democracy in their political system, but unfortunately, countries like Pakistan, Ghana, Burma, and others were not able to cope with the pressure exerted by internal and external forces, because of weak structural arrangements in the political system and they changed over to the authoritarian form, putting an end to parliamentary democracy. This switch-over was explained as an attempt to tackle internal forces which were at work against national unity. This argument was centred in the view that schismatic internal group activities were directed against the central authority of the political system[19], which naturally led to the patent follow up action by the central authority.

Among the nations in the Asian region, India is one of the few countries which are able to continue with the democratic structure in spite of threats of both internal and external forces. India has been rightfully called a subcontinent, which is massive in its area and population. Hence it faces numerous issues of several kinds, including geo-political ones. India has been rightly described as an ethnological museum consisting of several regions, races, languages, cultures and religions. This has inescapably led to internal incohesiveness among regional, lingual and caste groups. The national government attempts to mitigate the problem by adopting various strategies ranging from extending small economic concessions to military action to suppress group activities. Equally the groups are also exerting their pressure on the government by positing their demands ranging from small socio-economic concessions to the attainment of autonomous statehood. This process of the groups' interaction with the national government and the response of the national government to the groups is construed as a threat to national unity and scholars tend to take an alarmist perspective of the whole process. But the perspective of the present work varies sharply from the established views, which fall into a pattern. The groups which demand more allocation of funds as well rights for the respective regions exhibit only their participating political culture which, if rightly channelised, will pave the way for nation building rather than disintegration. The regional groups are keen and alert in getting the maximum share in the national allocation. At the same time, these groups have proved themselves active in supporting the nation during the hour of crisis[20]. The groups which put forth secessionist demands are not really anti-national. On a close and unbiased scrutiny one can perceive that their demands by themselves are not important to them. They employ them only as instruments for gaining political power and it is a rather uncharitable approach to regard them as disintegrating forces at all. Further, it is a matter of common observation that people who are loyal to their race, community and religion are more loyal to the state than many others in building the nation and preserving the unity of the country.

The Problem

In India, since the formation of the states, several federal units, namely Punjab, Kashmir, Tamil Nadu, Nagaland, Mizoram and Assam have been continuously fighting for their group demands and for their local interests. These forces have been adopting several methods to achieve their goals. All these methods have always been considered by the state authorities detrimental to the unity of the country. But the author of this work feels that the forces which are fighting for group demands for decentralization of power or state autonomy will not become forces of national disintegration. On the contrary they help the central authority to save the country from disaster and disintegration during the time of crisis much more than the forces which are generally considered to be loyal to the central authority[21]. Since the people of these regions are more aware and active in the functioning of the political system, they seek more rights for achieving their demands, for which they fight continuously by adopting a number of strategies. These strategies could never be ends in themselves, but only the means to achieve their ends. It is against this background that the present study is attempted. This study aims to analyse the loyalty of the people of Tamil Nadu towards the ethnic group and the nation. Tamil Nadu is here considered as a strong unit playing a vital role in the process of province building by posting demands like an independent Dravidasthan and state autonomy for Tamil Nadu. It is an appropriate case for analysis of loyalty. Though the Tamils have fought for ethnic demands through their ethnic political party (Dravida Munnetra Kazhagam) they have contributed substantially to the nation building process. At the same time they continue to pose the same demands such as asking for more powers for thc regional government and state autonomy. Hence there is a possibility of a strong permise that an ethnic group can have multiple loyalty. People of an ethnic group can have loyalty towards the ethnic group and the nation simultaneously. Intensity of loyalty may have variations. Therefore the present study attempts to analyse the loyalty of the people of Tamil Nadu towards the nation and the ethnic group or organisation. This study will answer the following questions:

(i) What are the demands of the groups from the central authority?
(ii) In what circumstances do ethnic organisations project their goals?
(iii) What are the means adopted to realise their goals?
(iv) How do generations transmit the demands?
(v) What are the changes in their demands over generations?
(vi) How do they keep their relationship with the group, and the nation?
(vii) How do they exhibit their loyalty towards either the nation or the ethnic group?
(viii) Do the ethnic demands matter at all?

Review of Literature

In the recent years a number of schools have attempted to study national loyalty in different countries[22]. These works have analysed the reasons for the loyalty of the people towards the central authority of the state and towards the regions, how this process has been interchanged, how people are shifting and changing their loyalty over a period of time, and, the causes for the shift of loyalty. In almost all the works, they have extensively analysed the modernization effect on the process of nation-building and integrating the segmented communities. They have tried to evolve a meaningful theory and a model which would relate the impact of modernization to integrating the communities but in vain. But, in the context of India, a few studies have appeared[23]. These studies have analysed the problems in the process of building the nation from the perspective of the state. However this issue has not been analysed from the point of view of the people. Joseph W. Elder in his article[24] evaluated the level of national loyalty of the people towards the central authority. He has selected two villages and towns from Madurai district in Tamil Nadu and Lucknow district in Uttar Pradesh as units of the study. Despite the novelty of the exercise to study the loyalty of the people in the two places, it suffers from certain limitations. Its sampling procedure is of doubtful validity which does not permit generalization at any significant level. Further it lacks adequate indepth analysis, particularly of the factor of loyalty. The present studies tries to fill the gap that exists on the theme of group loyalty to ethnicity and the nation.

Theory at Hand

The theory of mankind has always been related to the identification of the self with a group or organisation. The self identification may primarily be determined by certain symbols which tend to vary from period to period and area to area[25]. So it is very difficult to fix the anchorage of the identity of oneself either in the context of time or space with anyone of the symbols which normally tune the instinct of the human being to mark his or her placement to satisfy socio-economic and political needs. Thus identification of oneself or identity is a swing move from one end to another in a continnum[26]. Further more, it has many dimensions, and, at a point of time, human beings are identified with different objects, analytically called symbols, and, through identification they extend loyalty to different objects and realise their material benefits mostly and, at times, psychological satisfaction too. This fluctuating identity and loyalty has been described and analysed by historians, anthropologists, sociologists, economists, psychologists, political scientists from the past to the present in various terms.

At present, two important concepts, ethnicity and nationalism, confront the researchers in the disciplines of social science for a meaningful discourse to understand the reality of the movement of social phenomena[27]. The two concepts have been extensively researched by the scholars in the modern context in different connotations, namely, nation-building, state building, province building, nationalism, sub-nationalism, ethno-nationalism, ethnicity, ethnic identity, ethnocentrism, regionalism, cultural nationalism, communalism and tribalism[28].

It is evident from the proliferation of literature in form of books and journals and from the organising of research institutes at national and international levels that adequate attention has been given to this issue[29]. However still perplexing questions need clarification, explanation and justification. Some of the questions are: Can there be congruence between ethnic identity and national loyalty? Will they work mutually or will they work oppositely? If they work mutually in a continuum, what will be the result of their interaction? These questions are addressed and analysed here in the light of the existing theories on nationalism and ethnicity.

It will be very difficult to traverse over the entire gamut of the theories developed on nationalism and ethnicity. But a glimpse of the more celebrated theoretical works will provide the perspective to take up a scientific investigation and logical explanation of the problem. Scholars engaged in the analysis of nationalism and ethnicity invariably refer to *Nationalism and Social Communication: An Inquiry into the Foundations of Nationalism*[30] by Karl W. Deutsch. Evidently, it passes for a classic of this century in the field. It is Deutsch who triggered the research endeavour in this area by formulating the proposition that the problems persisting in the Nation-States in terms of fissiparous tendencies will wither away as modernization progress. Subsequently, however, his basic premise was disputed by scholars[31] who projected a new trend to the effect that modernization creates cleavages in the society and, consequently, the whole state system has to work for managing the ethnic groups[32]. It followed suit that interested academics, mostly from Sociology, Political Science and Psychology extensively analysed the ethnic factors and their linkages with scientific state system. The primary causative factors for the formation of groups on ethnic lines have been adequately explored[33], the strategies, symbols, identities of the groups have also been examined; and, frameworks have been evolved[34]. An equally vigorous analysis has been made to identify the strategies adopted by the scientific state system to bring all those groups which profess ethnicity under the common rubric of the Nation-State. Technically the points where the groups and the state meet and the groups assimilate with the mainstream, and where the ethnic groups turn to be non-malleable or move towards separation or proclaiming independence, have also been examined by adopting various theoretical frameworks[35].

Model to Explain

However a well conceived model is not at hand to explain what we need to explain. The guidelines provided by Chew Sock Foon, in his article[36] enable us to codify a suitable model to explain the congruence of the identities and the loyalties of an ethnic group in a scientific state system to develop itself. The basic assumption of the model is that identification is a process by which very individual identifies himself or herself with a group on a shared value and understanding the reality to maximise his/her benefit in the authoritative allocation of values in the economic, social and political spheres. Identity does not remain fixed on a particular value or symbol or instrument

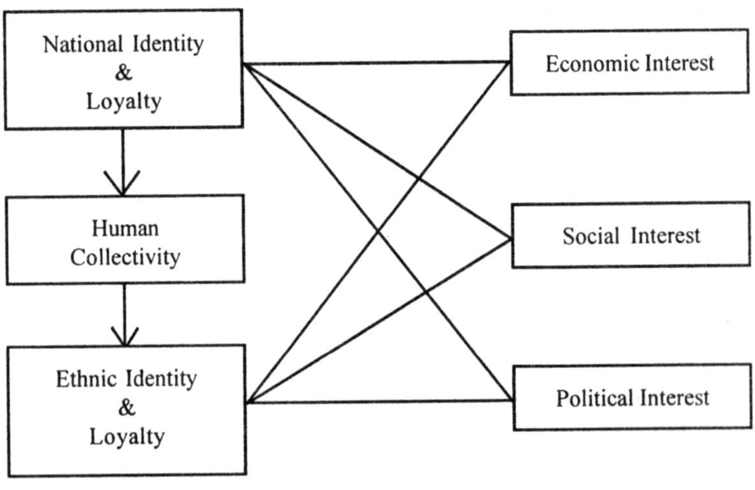

A Simple Model of Multiple Identity and Loyalty

for long. Moreover, any individual might have more than one identity and multiple identities and the anchorage of the identity depends on the interest with which the person identifies with values[37].

Human collectivity is organised on some common values and understanding to realise their dream in the life. At present, the Nation-State is the supreme legitimate political institution to fulfil the aspirations of the human collectivities. Naturally every individual in a Nation-State must owe allegiance to the nation first. But, in reality, keeping quite in a scientific state system by human collectivity does not solve any problem and it is the responsibility of the individual to project the demands through an organised group to settle or solve the problems. In such a context, the people try to discover symbols to bring the individual under a common banner. It could be done through either colour or race or religion or language or culture or region or community or tribe. By and large, categorization of human collectivity is commonly done under ethnic groups. Despite the fact that the groups are organised on ethnic lines, the concept of "nation" has not lost its significance. It has, on the contrary, received prominence[38], because the whole developmental process of society is the result of the interaction between the state and the ethnic groups. In the process of interaction the groups will gradually get some of their social, political and economic demands met and, in turn, the groups will change the intensity of their feeling or identity both in terms of nation and ethnicity. In the cyclical process, a group will transform its identity several times to suit its requirements. Likewise and ethnic group may have loyalty towards the nation with varying intensity. Therefore it is proposed to adopt this model to analyse the identity and loyalty of an ethnic group (Tamils in India) in this study. Based on the above explained model and the theories reviewed earlier a few objectives have been formulated. They are as given hereunder:

Objectives

1. To study the political, social and cultural identity of the people of Tamil Nadu.

2. To analyse the causes for the formation of the identity of the people of Tamil Nadu.
3. To analyse the level of loyalty of the people of Tamil Nadu towards the central authority (state).
4. To analyse the level of loyalty of the people of Tamil Nadu towards the regional ethnic group or ethno-nationalism.
5. To study the relationship between socio-political communication and the loyalty of the people towards the state or nation and ethnic group.
6. To study the changes between generations in national loyalty and ethnic group loyalty.

Hypothesis

1. The loyalty of the people towards ethno-nationalism is a function of the policies of the central authority and objective conditions of state building.
2. The higher the loyalty of the people towards ethno-nationalism the greater is the loyalty of the people towards the state (central authority) or nation.
3. The change of generations in the political system results in change of perceptions about the demands and pursuits of ethnic groups and the behaviour of the state.

Methodology

To test the above stated hypotheses, parameters for loyalty have been identified. Anthony D. Smith, who has worked extensively on nationalism and ethnicity has listed six characteristics of an ethnic[39]. Based on the characteristics, traits have been fixed. From the traits, indicators of loyalty have been fixed. Indicators of loyalty towards ethnic group and indicators of loyalty towards the nation have been fixed. Fifteen traits have been identified as indicators of ethnic loyalty and seven traits have been fixed as indicators of national loyalty. The following are the ethnic traits: attachment to mother-tongue (Tamil), equating mother-tongue (Tamil) with mother-preference for Tamil; giving importance to Tamil calendar of activities; celebrating Tamil festivals; sending wards to Tamil medium schools; demanded recognition for Tamil as a classical language; demanding ownership of property only for Tamils in Tamil Nadu; achieving development through Tamil; looking at issues from the perspective of Tamil tradition; giving importance to agitation against imposition of Hindi; perpetuating the feeling of deprivation; cultivating faith in ethnic political parties; and, Tamilising the polity of Tamil Nadu. The following are the seven national traits: identifying with Nation-State; actively supporting the Nation-State during times of crisis by extending moral and material support; respecting national symbols; supporting the central government during times of dispute between the centre and the state government; recognising the services rendered by national leaders; always participating in national celebrations; and preferring national identity. All the indicators have been incorporated as questions in the interview schedule designed. Data have been collected from the basic records relating to electoral participation, policies of the central authority towards the demands of the ethnic group and reaction of the people to these policies. Regarding the loyalty of the people, a properly conceived well-structured schedule has been administered. The schedule consists of five parts, namely the socio-economic background of the respondents, political socialisation of the respondents, political participation of the respondents, ethnic identity of the respondents and national loyalty of the respondents. To elicit information regarding all aspects of loyalty one hundred questions have been set in the schedule.

Sample Design

The author have to keep in view the fact that industrialization and modernization are the major factors influencing the loyalty of the people. Considering these are the bases of stratification, all the taluks of the state were classified under two divisions: (i) Industrialized and Modernized; and (ii) Non-Industrialized and Non-Modernized. On a random basis two taluks from each division were first selected.

At the next stage, from the four taluks, eight villages were chosen, At the rate of two from each taluk. Each set of the two categories of villages represent the strongholds of the national parties and regional parties. The details of the areas chosen for this study are given hereunder:

Respondents are drawn from the areas mentioned hereunder

District	*District*
Ramanathapuram (Non-Industralised)	Coimbatore (Industiralised)
Blocks	*Blocks*
Keelakkarai	Mettupalayam
Mandapam	Udumalpet
Kamuthi	Thirupoor
Muthukulathoor	Valparai
Towns	*Towns*
Aranmanai	Gandhipuram
Bharathi Nagar	Ukkadam
Sethupathi Nagar	Bharathi Nagar
Earvadi	Perur
Uchipuli	Serayampalayam
Rameshwaram	Govai Pudur
Abiramam	R. K. Puram
Thondi	Karamadai
Thiruvadanai	Periyanegamam
	Avinasi
	K. Pudur
	Paladam
Villages	*Villages*
Kodikulam	Somanur
Kenikarai	Sarkar
Pothagavayal	Periyanayallan Palayam
Madhavanoor	Sirumugai
Thirupulani	Pogaloor
Sakkarakottai	Kovanoor

Villages

Madathakulam
Mayankulam
Vedalai
Panaikulam
Chinnapalam
Akkamadam
Pudumadam
Earakadu
Thanuskodi
Pandiyarajanpuram
Makindi
Parthibanoor
Melapanaiyur
Thelichathanallur
Perunali
Melakodumalur
Ponvasal
Kadladi
Sambakulam
Pamboor
Muthanari
Mangalakudi
Ananthoor
Sarukani
Oriyur
Nambukalai

Villages

Palaya Pudur
Arthanaripalayam
Vellore
Thirumoorthy Nagar
Thali
Madathakulam
Kanchanpatti
Manupatti
Kattampatti
Ramapattinam
Nayakkanpalayam
Kenathukadavu
Singanallur
Soolakkal
Kovindapuram
Perumanallur
Kandiyan Kovil
Nallur
Veerapandi
Marathi Palayam
Parmbikulam
Kalalyanpanthal

Next a 10 per cent sample of the households of the chosen villages categorised according to occupational groupings were identified in a random manner. These households were administered the interview schedule in an interview setting. Thus a three-layered random sampling was adopted for this study.

Relevance and Significance of the Study

Different ethnic groups raise their demands with the central authority and sometimes the groups make even extreme demands such as separate statehood to achieve their group demands but their basic intention is not to disturb the unity of the nation. It is misconstrued and misinterpreted that these ethnic groups are posing serious threats to the nation by way of voicing their demands. It is observed that during national crises, the ethnic groups which pose such serious demands strongly support the nation by contributing more liberally to the cause of the state (central authority) than the other groups which do not pose any serious demands to the nation. Hence these groups, which demand due rights for their states (provinces) and hence are deemed to be separatists, could be studied with a view to analysing their loyalty towards the central authority and the ethnic group. At present, it is a vital topic for politicians as well as academicians and it will stimulate a new thinking in the direction of working for national integration. This study could be considered a pioneering endeavour to gain a precise and clear picture of the thinking of the people about the state and nation.

NOTES AND REFERENCES

1. Nathan Glazer and Danier Patrick Moynihan, *Beyond the Melting Pot,* Massachusetts: The MIT Press, 1963.
2. Greeley, *Ethnicity in the United States: A Preliminary Reconnaissance,* New York: Willey, 1974.
3. W. Connor, "Nation Building or Nation Destroying," *World Politics* 24:3 (1972).
4. A.P. Royce, *Ethnic Identity : Strategies of Diversity,* Bloomington: Indiana University Press,-1982.
5. D.L. Horowitz, *Ethnic Groups in Conflict,* Los Angeles: University of California Press, 1985.
6. D.L. Thompson and Ronen Dov (eds.) *Ethnicity, Politics and Development,* Colorado: Lynne Rienner Publishers, 1966.
7. Joseph Rothschild, *Ethnopolitics: A Conceptual Framework,* New York: Colombia University Press, 1981.
8. Fred W. Riggs, *Ethnicity: International Conceptual Encyclopaedia for the Social Sciences,* Vol. 1, UNESCO, 1985.

9. M.J. Esmen (ed.), *Ethnic Conflict in the Western World,* New York: Cornell University Press, 1977.

10. S.N. Eisenstadt and S. Rokkan (eds.), *Building States and Nations,* Vol. II, Beverley Hills: Sage Publications, 1973.

11. Karl W. Deutsch and Foltz (eds.), *Nation Building,* New York: Atherton, 1966.

12. W. Connor, "The Politics of Ethno-Nationalism", *Journal of International Affairs* 27: 1 (1975).

13. Karl W. Deutsch, "Social Mobilisation and Political Development", *American Political Science Review,* (September) 1961.

14. G. Palanithurai, "Ethnic Leader and Social Change: A Study in Micro Modelling", *Journal of Annamalai University PART A (Humanities),* Vol. 33 (1987).

15. D.J. Grove, "A Test of the Ethnic Equalization Hypothesis: A Cross-National Study", *Ethnic and Racial Studies,* 1:2 (1978).

16. G. Palanithurai, *Management of Ethnic Conflict in India and Canada,* New Delhi: Kanishka Publishers and Distributors, 1995.

17. J.M. Yinger, "Towards a Theory of Assimilation and Dissimilation", *Ethnic and Racial Studies,* 1:4 (1981).

18. W. Connor, "A nation is a nation, is a state; is an ethnic group, is a ....", *Ethnic and Racial Studies,* 4:3 (1978).

19. Joseph W. Elder, "National Loyalties in a Newly Independent Nation," in *Ideology and Discontent* (ed.), David Apter, London: The Free Press of Glencoe, 1954, p.77.

20. Loyalty of the groups could be measured in terms of their monetary contribution to the central authority and supportive measures in tackling national crisis by supporting the national government.

21. Dravida Munnetra Kazhagam (DMK) is an ethnic political party which posed ethnic demands to the national government with force ever since its inception and at the same time, whenever the nation faced a crisis, it supported the national government in tackling the crisis. For instance, during the Indo-China War in 1962, the party gave up its demand of secession and on another occasion, during the Indo-Pakistan war, this party liberally donated a huge sum to the national government as war fund. More so, on both the occasions they conducted a large number of public meetings to mobilize the people in support of the national government. See: S. Bhaskaran, "Issues in Federalism : Problem of National Integration in Indian and Canadian Federal Systems — A Research Design," presented at the Indo-Canadian Workshop at Hyderabad, 1981.

22. Karl W. Deutsch, *Nationalism and Social Communication* (Cambridge, Mass, 1956); Thomas Hodgkin, *Nationalism in Colonial Africa* (New York, 1957); James Coleman, *Nigeria: Background to Nationalism* (Berkeley, 1958); Danial Lerner, *The Passing of Traditional Society* (New York, 1985); R. Emerson, *From Empire to Nation* (Cambridge, Mass, 1960); Hans Kohn, *The Idea of Nationalism* (New York, 1961); S.M. Lipset, *First New Nation* (New York, 1963); Fred Vonder Mehden, *Religion and Nationalism in South East Asia* (Madison, 1963); Williard A. Beling and George O. Tolten, eds., *Developing Nations: Quest for a Model* (New York, 1970); and Philip E. Jacob and James V. Toscano (eds.), *The Integration of Political Communities* (Philadelphia, 1964).

23. Rajni Kothari, "Integration and Performance: Two Pivots of India's Model of Nation Building" in *State and Nation Building: A Third World Perspective* (ed.), Rajni Kothari (New Delhi : Allied Publishers Private Limited, 1976); Ainslie T. Embree, "Pluralism and National Integration: The Indian Experience," *Journal of International Affairs,* 27:1 (1973).

24. Joseph W. Elder, *op. cit.*

25. C. H. Enloe, *Ethnic Conflict and Political Development,* Boston: Little Brown and Company, 1973; D.L. Thomson and D. Roness (eds.), *Ethnicity, Politics and Development,* Colorado, Lynne Riesnei Publishers, 1986; G. Palanithurai, "Ethnicity and Development: A New Formation," paper presented at 46th Conference of Indian Political Science Association at Pune from 3rd to 5th November, 1989.

26. A.P. Royee, *Ethnic Identity: Strategies of Diversity,* Bloomington : Indiana University Press, 1982.

27. P. Brass (ed.) *Ethnic Groups and the State,* London : Croom Helm, 1985; H. Seton-Watson, *Nations and States,* London: Methuen, 1977; A.D. Smith, *State and the Nation in the Third World,* Brighton: Harvester Press, 1983.

28. In order to dispel the misunderstanding and non-understanding of the concept pertinent to ethnicity, a glossary has been prepared under the editorship of Fred W. Riggs. See the meaning of the concepts in Fred W. Riggs, *Ethnicity: International Conceptual Encyclopaedia for the Social Sciences,* Vol. I, Published under the auspices of the International Social Science Council, Committee on Conceptual and Terminological Analysis (COCTA).

29. J. Yinger, "Ethnicity in Complex Societies : Structural, Cultural and Characterological Factors," in L. Coses and O. Larsen (eds.), *The Uses of Controversy in Sociology,* New York: Free Press, 1976.

30. K.W. Deutsch, *Nationalism and Social Communication,* 2nd Edition, New York: MIT Press, 1966.

31. Judith Nagata, "The Status of Ethnicity and Ethnicity of Status," *International Journal of Comparative Sociology,* Vol. 17, No. 3-4, 1976, pp. 242-260; Martion O. Heisler, "Ethnic Conflict in the World Today," *The Annals of the American Academy of Political and Social Sciences,* No. 433, 1977; E. Burgess, "The Resurgence Ethnicity of Myth or Reality?", *Ethnic and Racial Studies,* Vol. 1, No. 3, 1978; Cannor Walker, "Nation Building or Nation Destroying?", *World Politics,* Vol. 20, No. 3, 1972.

32. Thomas Remeikis, "Modernization and National Identity in the Baltic Republics: Uneven and Multi-Directional Change in the Components of Modernization," in Ihor Kamenetsky (ed.), *Nationalism and Human Rights: Process of Modernization in the USSR,* Littleton: Lievaries Unlimited Inc., 1977.

33. Malcolm Cross, "Colonialism and Ethnicity, a Theory and Comparative Case Study," *Ethnic and Racial Studies,* Vol. I, No. 1, 1978, pp. 37-59; Micheal Hechter and Margeret Levi, "The Comparative Analysis of Ethnoregional Movement," *Ethnic and Racial Studies,* Vol. 2, No.3, 1979, pp. 260-274; E. Burgess, "The Resurgence of Ethnicity, Myth or Reality?," *Ethnic and Racial Studies,* Vol. 1, No. 3, 1978; Donald L. Horowitz, "Patterns of Ethnic Separatism," *Comparative Studies in Society and History,* Vol. 23, No. 2, 1981, pp. 174-178; E. Sagrin and James Moneymaker, "Language Nationalist Movement," in R. Hall (ed.), *Ethnic Autonomy Comparative Dynamics,* New York: Pergamon Press, 1979, pp. 18-37.

34. For this see the exhaustive reference in Joseph Rothschild, *Ethnopolitics: A Conceptual Framework,* New York : Columbia University Press, 1981.

35. C.H. Enloe, "Internal Colonialism, Federalism and Alternative State Development Strategies," *Publics,* Vol. 7, No. 4, 1977, pp. 145-160; James Lightbody, "A Note on the Theory of Nationalism as a Function of Ethnic Demands," *Canadian Journal of Political Science,* Vol. 2, No. 3, 1969, pp. 327-337; L.S. Mckinsey, "Dimensions of National Political Integration and Disintegration: The Case of Quebec Separatism 1960-75," *Comparative Political Studies,* Vol. 9, No. 3, 1976, pp. 335-360.

36. C.S. Foon, "On the Incompacability of Ethnic and National Loyalties: Reframing the Issue," *Canadian Review of Studies in Nationalism,* Vol. III, No. 1, 1986, pp. 1-2.

37. Frederick Barath, *Ethnic Groups and Boundaries,* Boston: Little Brown and Company, 1969; Peter D. Preez, *The Politics of Identity: Ideology and the Human Image,* Oxford: Basil Blackwell, 1980.

38. A.D. Smith, "The Myth of the Modern Nation and the Myths of Nations," *Ethnic and Racial Studies,* Vol. II, No. 1, 1988, pp. 1-25.

39. A.D. Smith, *The Ethnic Origins of Nations,* Oxford : Blackwell, 1986.

2

SOCIO-ECONOMIC BACKGROUND

One of the earliest approaches to the study of group behaviour was the analysis of socio-economic characteristics of the group[1]. The political activities of an individual in a group and that of the group in the political institution are always influenced by the socio-demographic characteristics of the individuals and the collectivities. The socio-economic characteristics of the individuals and groups have a bearing on the dynamic process of the political institutions irrespective of the nature of the society. Generally while considering the political activities of an individual in a group and of the group in the political process, one has to notice two options, namely: (*a*) the impact of socio-demographic characteristics of the individuals on the political activities, and (*b*) the cumulative effect of the socio-demographic characteristics of the individuals on the functioning of the political institutions. Notwithstanding the differences between the developed society and the developing society, the socio-economic conditions do play an important and significant part in the political process of any society[2]. Individuals vary in the exercise of their power. Equally the influence of individuals on the political process varies. Though the Constitution has established equal rights, while influencing the government, individuals realise different levels of influence on the political process. Whether it is Karl Marx or Max Weber, this convention has no gainsay. Hence, it is essential to project the socio-economic background of the respondents. Socio-economic background comprises many variables of which education, occupation, income, wealth and caste are important categories. Each variable has its own significance in influencing the dyanamic process of the political institutions. Against this backdrop, a detailed description of the socio-economic background of the respondents is essential and therefore it is given in this chapter.

Before proceeding with the description of the socio-economic background of the individuals, it would be appropriate to indicate the details of the age group of the respondents. In order to get the opinion of the people, different age groups have been contacted in this study.

Age is a factor which has its own implication in the dynamic process of the social and political systems. Age and influence and age and power go hand-in-hand. For political socialization and political requirement, age does contribute its might[3]. As the Dravidian Movement has its genesis, growth, development and change in different periods, it is essential that the respondents be grouped according to their age to get their reflection on politics based on their experience in different periods. Perception, behaviour and performance of the respondents vary from one age group to another. Hence age was considered as a factor in the analysis of group and identity formation in this work.

Table 2.1 : Distribution of Respondents by Age

Sl. No.	Category	No. of Respondents	Percentage
1.	20 - 30	54	13.50
2.	31 - 40	123	30.75
3.	41 - 50	182	45.50
4.	51 & Above	41	10.25
	Total	400	100.00

Source : Computed.

Among the respondents, around 75 per cent are in the age group of thirty-one to fifty. The respondents of this age group might be politically socialised and well-disposed towards political issues. When the Dravidian Movement was in the thick of the political system, this age group was socialised politically on ethnic issues. During the 60s and 70s, through the creation of a number of reading centres in the rural areas by the DMK, the people were educated politically through the writings of the stalwarts of the Dravidian Movement.

Table 2.2 : Distribution of Respondents by Sex

Sl. No.	Category	No. of Respondents	Percentage
1.	Male	351	87.75
2.	Female	49	12.75
	Total	400	100.00

Source : Computed.

Next to age, sex is an another important variable in the study of socio-economic background related to the dynamic process of political institutions. It was decided to have 50 per cent of the respondents from the female category. But the research associate's attempt to get 50 per cent of women respondents was futile and so, 87 per cent of the respondents are male in this study. The Dravidian Movement advocated the liberation and emancipation of women. Yet contacting women in the family for interaction is very difficult even among the families of the members of the Dravidian Movement.

In Indian society, generally, excepting the higher echelons. women have a traditional role and they do not enjoy freedom and liberty in their households in deciding their political preferences and options as men do[4]. It was the Dravidian Movement which struggled hard to work for the emancipation of women. In Tamil Nadu women have been equated with earth and God and culturally they are known for their compassion and tenderness. Hence they are portrayed as a segment which deserves special treatment as if they are weak and meek[5]. Even after fifty years of continuous work of the forces of the Dravidian Movement, the condition of the women in the rural areas has not changed or improved[6]. Hence sex as a variable plays an important role in deciding the process of Tamil polity.

Table 2.3 : Distribution of Respondents by Education

Sl. No.	Category	No. of Respondents	Percentage
1.	Illiterate	12	3.00
2.	Primary	103	25.75
3.	Secondary	186	46.50
4.	College	71	17.75
5.	Others	28	7.00
	Total	400	100.00

Source : Computed.

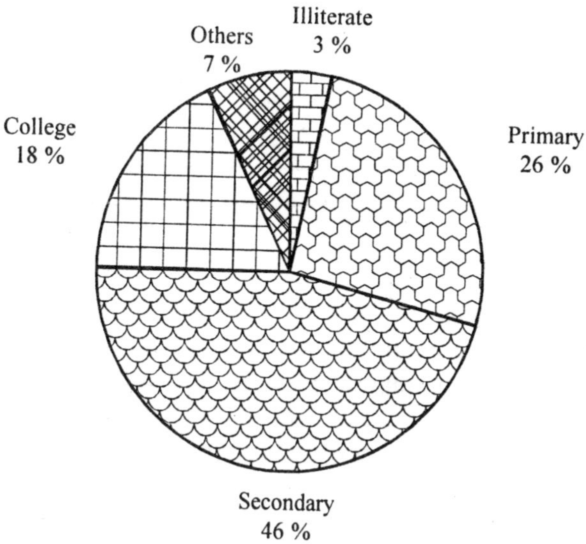

Fig. 2.1 : Distribution of Respondents by Education

The Dravidian Movement is known for its activities aimed at reating awareness among the people about their backwardness. 'hey highlighted the backwardness of the people and the resons for ieir backwardness. They emphasised the importance of literacy nd they also motivated the mumbers of the movement to educate ll. In fact, the Dravidian Movement started its activities with ducation. To educate the people, hundreds of village reading rooms were created by the liberal contributions of the people. In the past three decades, as emphasised by the Dravidian Movement, education has been given importance and, as a result, there is considerable improvement in the field of education and employment[7] : 71 per cent of the respondents have had primary and secondary education; 17 per cent have had collegiate education; and only 3 per cent are illiterate.

Table 2.4 : Distribution of Respondents by Occupation

Sl. No.	Category	No. of Respondents	Percentage
1.	Agriculture	127	31.75
2.	Business	111	27.75
3.	Industries	42	10.50
4.	Teachers	86	21.15
5.	Others	34	8.50
	Total	400	100.00

Source : Computed.

Next to education, occupation has its own bearing on th perception of the people. In the Indian context occupation o individuals plays an important role in determining the social an economic status. Once social status is decided and determined, th individual's influence in society and polity can be easily gauged. O most occasions, occupations are not chosen by the individuals o their own and they are decided by the social structure based on th tradition. The Dravidian Movement has questioned even the bas concept of the traditional occupation of the families, individua and castes[8]. As a result one can find a major shift in the occupatic of families in Tamil society in the last three decades. Hence it necessary to understand the occupational background of tl respondents. Of the respondents 59 per cent are agriculturists ar small business owners. Next to them are teachers who played key role in the emergence of the Dravidian Movement. Both tl agriculturists and the businessmen are not very rich and they enga in these professions as they have been bequeathed to them by their ancestors. About 10 per cent of the respondents are industrialists and they are also not so rich, but belong to middle class families.

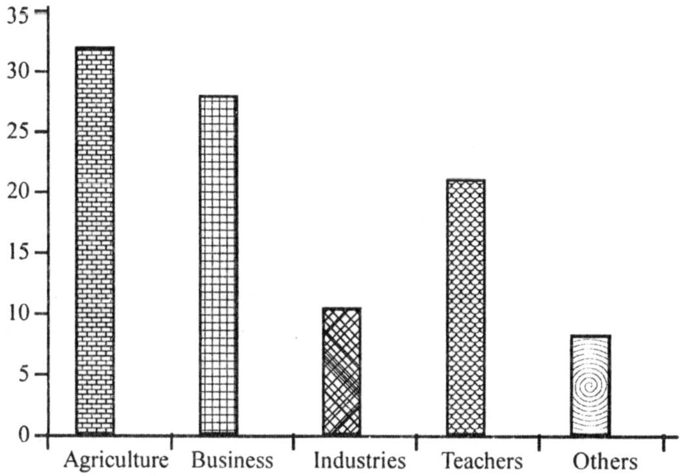

Fig 2.2 : Distribution of Respondents by Occupation

Table 2.5 : Distribution of Respondents by Annual Income

Sl. No.	Category	No. of Respondents	Percentage
1.	0 - 20,000	109	27.25
2.	20,001 - 40,000	173	43.25
3.	40,001 - 60,000	66	16.50
4.	60,001 & Above	52	13.00
	Total	400	100.00

Source : Computed.

The income of the respondent has a bearing on his or her activities in the socio-political sphere. But it is very difficult to assess the exact position of the respondents' status by income in the Indian context. People provide data advantageous to them[9]. Yet, we have to rely on them. It is seen in Table 2.5 that 27 per cent of the respondents have an annual income of upto Rs. 20,000; 43 per cent have an income of between Rs. 20,001 and 40,000 per annum; and poor and middle income group are more in number among the respondents. The income of the respondents is one of the factors in determining the economic background of the respondents.

Table 2.6 : Distribution of Respondents by Wealth Status

Sl. No.	Category	No. of Respondents	Percentage
1.	0 - 1,00,000	97	13.50
2.	1,00,001 - 2,00,000	213	53.25
3.	2,00,000 & Above	90	22.50
	Total	400	100.00

Source : Computed.

Wealth status is yet another difficult area for handling in social science research. People approximate the value of their properties. They calculate according to their understanding and assessment and this need not necessarily tally with the estimate of the government. Further, respondents who want to project their status as very high give inflated data. Of the respondents, 77 per cent belong to the category of not rich but belong to the poor and middle class. Only 22.5 per cent of the respondents belong to the upper middle class. The politics of the Dravidian Movement is primarily based on the activities of the middle class backward communities[10].

Table 2.7 : Distribution of Respondents by Community

Sl. No.	Category	No. of Respondents	Percentage
1.	Scheduled Caste	56	14.00
2.	Scheduled Tribe	3	0.75
3.	Most Backward Class	112	28.00
4.	Backward Class	171	42.75
5.	Forward Class	58	14.50
	Total	400	100.00

Source : Computed.

In Indian polity, the role of communities cannot be ignored. At present Indian polity is increasingly a communal one. But the intensity of the role varies from era to era. More specifically Tamil Nadu politics has been analysed from the perspective of caste from the formative years of Independence itself. The trend has picked up momentum in other states also. In the beginning it was just a caste- wise breakup into Backward Class, including the Dalits, Most Backward Classes and Brahmins. Now this broad classification has been broken up into sub-caste formations. In any social analysis one has to consider the role of the caste in the modern context. Of the respondents, 42.75 per cent belong to Backward Class, 28 per cent belong to Most Backward Classes and 15 per cent belong to SC and ST. They were the components of the Dravidian Movement once. Now each and every caste segment to the level of sub-caste has formed its own organisation to project its demands.

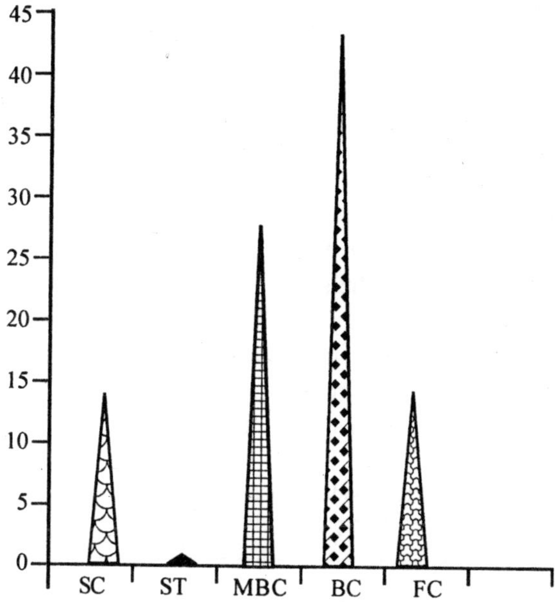

Fig. 2.3 : Distribution of Respondents by Community

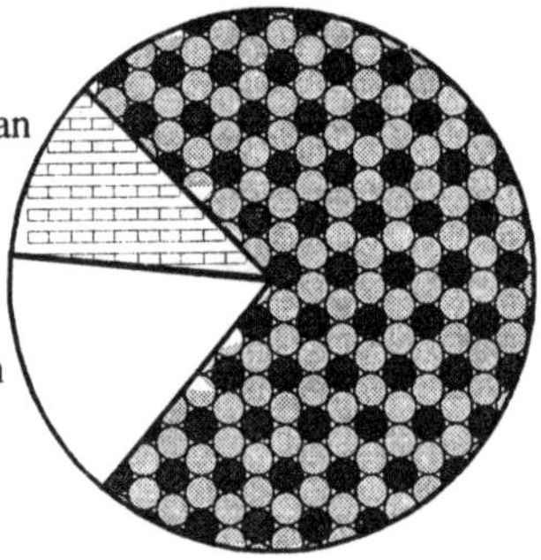

Fig. 2.4 : Distribution of Respondents by Religion

Table 2.8 : Distribution of Respondents by Religion

Sl. No.	Category	No. of Respondents	Percentage
1.	Hindu	288	72.00
2.	Muslim	70	17.50
3.	Christian	42	10.50
	Total	400	100.00

Source : Computed.

In the formative years of the Independence movement, it was community not religion which played a significant role in the political process of the nation and the state. There was conflict among the communities of the Hindu religion. The present day politics is hinges on religion and community simultaneously. It is seen in Table 2.8 that 72 per cent of the respondents are drawn from the Hindu segment, 17 per cent are Muslims and 10 per cent are Christians.

Table 2.9 : Distribution of Respondents by Settlement

Sl. No.	Category	No. of Respondents	Percentage
1.	Urban	187	46.75
2.	Rural	213	53.25
	Total	400	100.00

Source : Computed.

Initially the Dravidian Movement gained momentum in the urban areas and especially among the educated middle class of the backward communities. Gradually, because of the media, the movement extended to the rural areas also. Thus the ethnic movement had it anchorage in both urban and rural areas. For this study 53 per cent of the respondents are drawn from the rural areas and 47 per cent are drawn from the urban areas.

Individual affiliation with organisation plays an important role in determining the influence of the individual in the decision-making process. Individuals' decision on their affiliation with the organisation is an indicator of their commitment towards certain goals and targets. Hence the respondents' affiliations were elicited. Table 2.10 shows, about 60 per cent of the respondents have gone to caste organisations, while 11 per cent of the respondents have affiliated themselves with their professional organisations.

Table 2.10 : Distribution of Respondents by Membership in Organisation

Sl. No.	Category	No. of Respondents	Percentage
1.	Caste	61	59.80
2.	Trade	12	11.77
3.	Teachers	27	26.47
4.	Fans Club	2	1.96
	Total	102	100.00

Source : Computed.

On the whole 75 per cent of the respondents belong to the age group between 31 and 50. They would be vibrant and active players in politics. According to Table 2.2, 87 per cent of the respondents are men and only 13 per cent are women; 97 per cent of the respondents are educated and they are prone to active socialization process; agriculture, small trade, business and teaching are the predominant occupations of the respondents; 80 per cent of the respondents belong to the middle class; 85 per cent are from Backward, Most Backward and SC and ST Communities; only 15 per cent belong to the Forward Communities; 72 per cent of the respondents belong to Hindu religion, while 17 per cent are Muslims and 10 per cent are Christians. Thus the respondents belong to the middle class and the socially backward classes with reasonably good educational background. One could clearly see the implications of the socio-demographic background of the individuals for their socialization, perception, behaviour and performance.

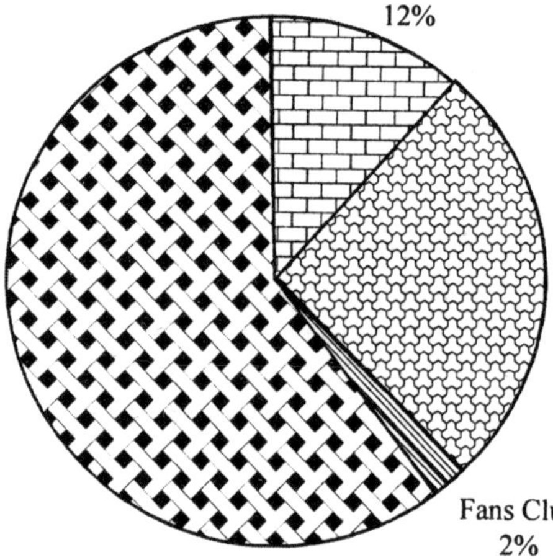

Fig. 2.5 : Distribution of Respondents by Membership in Organisation

NOTES AND REFERENCES

1. Sidney Verba, Norman H. Nie, Jae-on Kim, *Participation and Political Equality : A Seven Nation Comparison,* Cambridge: University Press, 1978, pp. 2-3.

2. G. Palanithurai *People's Perception of Politics: An Indian Perspective,* New Delhi: Kanishka Publishers and Distributors, 1995, p. 27.

3. James N. Schubert, Thomas C. Wiegele and Samuel M. Hines Jr, *Age, Age Structure and Political Decision-Making* [A Final Report to the National Institute of Aging] Dekalf : Northern Illinois University, 1986, pp. 1-29.

4. G. Palanithurai, "Ethnic Leader and Social Change: A Study in Micromodelling", *Journal of Annamalai University, Part A (Humanities).* Vol. 33 (1987), p. 89.

5. This has been extensively discussed by M.S.S. Pandian. See M.S.S. Pandian, *M.G. Ramachandran in Film and Politics: The Image Trap*, New Delhi: Sage Publications, 1992.
6. K. Veeramani, *Periyar on Women Rights*, Chennai : Emerald Publishers, 1994.
7. Madras Institute of Development Studies, *Tamil Nadu Economy: Performance and Issues*, New Delhi: Oxford & IBH Publishing Co Pvt. Ltd., 1988.
8. C.N. Annadurai, Varnasiram, Chennai: Parinilayam, 1978.
9. G. Palanithurai, *People's Participation of Politics: An Indian Perspective*, New Delhi: Kanishka Publishers and Distributors, 1995, p. 34.
10. Indhu Rajagopal, *The Tyranny of Caste: The Non-Brahmin Movement and Political Development in South India*, New Delhi: Vikas Publishing House, 1985.

3

POLITICAL SOCIALIZATION

After the outbreak of the behavioural revolution, behavioural studies in political science gained much currency and popularity among students and teachers. New areas have been adequately investigated and frameworks and models have been developed. Political culture, political recruitment, political behaviour, political mobilization, political participation and political socialization are some of the major areas which have drawn the attention of scholars[1]. Adequate exploratory and empirical studies have been carried out both in the first world and third world countries with liberal funding from agencies in the West. As a result abundant literature has been generated on the subject.

For a meaningful analysis of political participation, political recruitment, political mobilization and political behaviour, studying political socialization is imperative. Political socialization has been analysed under three distinct categories, namely (*a*) attachment to the political system, (*b*) political indoctrination, and (*c*) political participation[2]. Political socialization involves indoctrination, acculturation, civilising, cultural transmission and adopting cultural norms. Political socialization refers to the process of transformation of human groups in terms of acquiring political knowledge. It is nothing but a process by which people are oriented towards the political system and its sub-systems.

Attitudes, beliefs, views on political system are transmitted from one generation to another. It is presumed that the values and norms are transmitted from one generation to another and the transmission is carried out consciously to preserve the existing system. The question here is, how the concept of change is accounted for in the political process. Critics of political behaviour argue that political socialization has the distinct political function of maintaining stability. The general theory on political socialization stems from two major theoretical arguments. Individual dispositions are the primary output variables of interest and they form the way stations to the key output variables. Further, individual dispositions, beliefs and notions are changed by the active intervention of institutions. Institutional involvement in the process of socialization need not necessarily be always explicit and conscious. There are an array of institutions involved in the process of political socialization. They are family, educational institution, peer group, media, political party, professional organisation etc. This socialization is a two-way process. It is not mere learning. It is teaching also. This learning and teaching takes place at a great speed with political motives. It is a almost a natural law and an evolutionary process. But at a later stage political socialization proceeds with a sense of purpose and a large number of political institutions involve themselves consciously to orient the people.

Generally people are not oriented on their own in any ideology. As people from their early childhood have been in the society and interacting with the forces of the society for their development, they have been gaining notions about the ideas and institutions of the society. Hence, men's political orientation or social orientation or economic orientation starts from early childhood, dating from his day of consciousness about events and incidents. The process of orientation towards any ideology and institution is the outcome of the interplay of the agencies involved in the process and the basic desire of the individual. People are getting oriented because of the institutions involved and equally because the individuals have inclination towards the activities of the institutions.

Some institutions are always with the individuals and some institutions are far away from the individuals and yet they move closer to the people as the people desire to move closer to these institutions. The orientation of the people depends on the nature of the institutions involved in the process. So, it will be expedient to see here how people are oriented in the political process.

Table 3.1 : Distribution of Respondents by Membership in Organisations

Sl. No.	Category	No. of Respondents	Percentage
1.	Caste Association	61	59.80
2.	Trade Unions	12	11.77
3.	Teachers' Associations	27	26.47
4.	Fan Clubs	2	1.96
	Total	102	100.00

Source : Computed.

Before proceeding to analyze the role of the institutions, it is necessary to understand where the respondents are placed organization-wise, as this will give a clear picture of their orientation. Of the total four hundred respondents, only one hundred and two responded to the question on their membership in organisations. Others said that they have no strong organisational base. Any organisation takes a position for its functioning and hence it will orient its members to the values and norms that are required for its functioning. The members are consciously oriented towards the objectives of the organisation. Of the respondents who responded, around 60 per cent belong to caste associations. Their strong association with these organisations show the mindset of the people. They are in primordial consciousness and consciously seek self-interest. It is a paradox in Tamil Nadu, that despite the efforts of the Dravidian Movement towards the formation of language and cultural identity, of late, people are inclined towards a caste movement as they want to orient themselves on caste lines instead of on language and culture lines. This new identity formation indicates the drift of the people from the Dravidian Movement. In the formative years of the Dravidian Movement an array of newspapers and magazines were brought out by different organisations of the movement. Members of the Dravidian Movement were oriented in the ideology of the movement. After the ethnic political party (DMK) came to power, groups were formed to project the group interests. Group took different interests and identities. At this juncture strong caste groups emerged. These caste groups have started opposing the ethnic political parties for favouring only a few sections which belong to the middle class.

Next to membership of organisations, age at which individuals become aware of memorable political and social events is important because it is from that age that the individual's views and ideas have been formed. Naturally people start recognising events and incidents from the age of five or six. Concrete ideas are formed only during the teens. In the present study, it is inferred from the data that 45 per cent of the respondents became aware of politics between the ages of 21 and 25. That is, they were oriented in politics only at a late stage. In Tamil Nadu the political socialization process is always fast and continuous as ethnic political parties are actively involved in orienting the people in the concepts of nationalism and national integration. In the present case the respondents got to know about politics at the age of twenty-one to twenty-five. It to be noticed that after the ethnic political party came to power, it has not shown any interest in pursuing the same mobilization as it had done during 1960s and 1970s.

Table 3.2 : Age at which Respondents Acquired Awareness of Politics

Sl. No.	Category	No. of Respondents	Percentage
1.	5-10	13	3.25
2.	11-15	21	5.25
3.	16-20	74	18.50
4.	21-25	183	45.75
5.	26-30	52	13.00
6.	31 & Above	57	14.25
	Total	400	100.00

Source : Computed.

The political orientation has been affected by a number of agencies and of them political organisations, family and peer groups are more important. Table 3.3 reveals the nature of the institutions involved in the process of political socialization of the respondents.

Table 3.3 : Institutions Involved in Orientation of the People

Sl. No.	Category	No. of Respondents	Percentage
1.	Parents	11	2.75
2.	Friends	23	5.75
3.	Press	16	4.00
4.	Political Organisation	179	44.75
5.	Schoolmates	16	4.00
6.	Caste Leaders	77	19.25
7.	Teachers	21	5.25
8.	Politicians	57	14.25
	Total	400	100.00

Source : Computed.

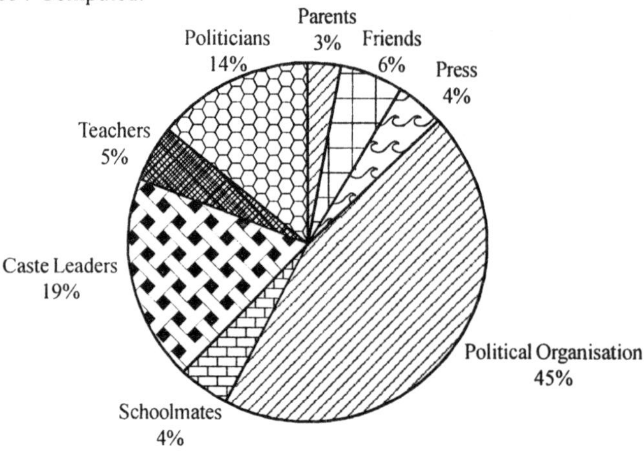

Fig. 3.1 : Institutions involved in Orientation of the People

Nearly 44 per cent of the respondents stated that they were oriented in politics by the involvement of political organisations. Next to political organisations, caste leaders were responsible for the orientation of the people in politics. At present two organisations are powerful in engendering identity among the people. They are caste organisations and political organisations. During the heyday of the Dravidian Movement it was only the ethnic political organisations which were powerful[3]. Over a period of three decades a sea change has occurred in the role of institutions in orienting the people. Caste organisations are more vibrant in socialising the people towards their objects[4]. Therefore members of political parties join caste organisations to gain benefits. Next to political organisations, the family plays a key role in socialising the individuals. In the Indian context, particularly, the family has a definite role in shaping the opinion of its members[5].

Table 3.4 : Family Member in Politics

Sl. No.	Category	No. of Respondents	Percentage
1.	Yes	117	29.25
2.	No	283	70.75
	Total	400	100.00

Source : Computed.

Only a minimum influence of the family is seen to work on the respondents as shown in Table 3.4. It may be due to non-affiliation of the family members to political organizations. As per Table 3.4, 70 per cent of the respondents' family members have no affiliation to political organizations. The respondents are freshers in politics. Hence, they have no strong roots in any political ideology. Yet, they may have strong preferences. In Indian polity one can notice the law of dynasty operating in party organizations by way of inducting the sons and daughters of politicians into politics[6]. Most of the sons and daughters of politicians are the junior politicians in the respective political parties or in other parties. This political identity transformation takes place in the family. However, in this study, majority of the respondents did not have family members in politics when they entered politics. They had no political forefathers.

Table 3.5 : Type of Newspaper Read

Sl. No.	Category	No. of Respondents	Percentage
1.	General Paper	187	46.75
2.	Party Paper	52	13.00
3.	Party & General	161	40.25
	Total	400	100.00

Source : Computed.

The media plays a key role in shaping the ideas of individuals in politics. A variety of newspapers and magazines have been published in the vernacular, providing a lot of information to the people. People have options to select papers. Depending on their interest individuals select newspapers: 46 per cent of the respondents are reading only general newspapers and magazines, while 40 per cent read both party and general newspapers. Only 13 per cent of the respondents read party newspapers. During 1950s and 1960s there were a large number of magazines published by the ethnic party leaders and organisations[7]. Those who identified with the ethnic organisations were the subscribers of the magazines. At present there is no such popular magazine. Now we have only party based newspapers. These are all symptoms of the decline of the mobilisation effort of the ethnic political organisations.

Table 3.6 : Friends with Political Affiliation

Sl. No.	Category	No. of Respondents	Percentage
1.	Yes	317	20.75
2.	No	83	79.25
	Total	400	100.00

Source : Computed.

Theoretically peer group influence is predominant on individuals. Hence one has to analyse the political affiliation of the peer group members. Nearly 79 per cent of the respondents have friends with political affiliation. There is every likelihood of the individuals who have political preferences to influence people to induct more number of members in the ethnic group. It is generally expected that the friends with political affiliation will influence the respondents also. It may be expected that the respondents having more chances for interaction with such friends will have a bearing on the perception of the respondents.

Table 3.7 : Community Members Involed in Politics

Sl. No.	Category	No. of Respondents	Percentage
1.	Yes	173	43.25
2.	No	227	56.75
	Total	400	100.00

Source : Computed.

Since Indian polity is caste oriented in nature, one has to look at every event against the backdrop of the social structure. Community leaders used to canvass for candidates at the time of election. Caste leaders have influence over their caste people. Hence, it is assessed whether the respondents' community leaders have active involvement in politics. As per Table 3.7, 56 per cent of the respondents have stated that their community members have no political involvement, while 43 per cent said that their community leaders are party oriented.

Table 3.8 : Political Experience During School Days

Sl. No.	Category	No. of Respondents	Percentage
1.	Yes	63	15.75
2.	No	337	84.25
	Total	400	100.00

Source : Computed.

Educational institutions constitute the key catalyst instrument in socialising individuals. It has been the practice in Tamil Nadu for all political parties, especially ethnic political parties, to establish their students wing in many of the popular and populous educational institutions. The ethnic political parties in Tamil Nadu established their stronghold among the students. The anti-Hindi agitation launched by the students in Tamil Nadu became an instrument for the ethnic political party to reach power at the state level[8]. But at present there is no such political fervour among the students and political parties have little inclination to organise the students for politics. Among the participants, only 16 per cent gained political experience during their school days as Table 3.8 shows.

Table 3.9 : Frequency of Discussion of Political Issues among Friends and Family Members

Sl. No.	Category	No. of Respondents	Percentage
1.	Frequently	58	14.50
2.	Occasionally	156	39.00
3.	Never	186	46.50
	Total	400	100.00

Source : Computed.

In the process of orientation of the respondents, the family plays a definite role, covertly or overtly influencing the individuals. Discussions take place, not necessarily consciously, among the members of the family about the political system or about the political events. Whether they are poor or rich, irrespective of their status, politics becomes a contentious issue in the interaction among the family members. Intensity of discussion varies from family to family. Of the four hundred respondents, only 15 per cent had frequent discussion in the family and friend's circle, while 39 per cent occasionally discussed political issues in their family and among their friends as Table 3.9 shows.

Generally, people discuss political issues during the time of election. For about two months, people will be mobilised by the parties through several activities during electioneering.

Table 3.10 : Practice of Influencing Family Members

Sl. No.	Category	No. of Respondents	Percentage
1.	Yes	119	29.75
2.	No	281	70.25
	Total	400	100.00

Source : Computed.

Some family members intentionally influence the members of the family politically. In the slow process of interaction, family members are oriented towards politics with involvement of the dominant members of the family. In the Indian context, the head of family or any male dominant member of the family used to influence the other members of the family. The Dravidian Movement adopted an unique method of socialising the member towards their movement. They organised periodical meetings and conferences to which families were invited and family functions were conducted with the involvement of the parties functionaries. Even in the conferences and meetings they were instructed to influence others and bring more number of families into the fold of the Dravidian ideology. This practice is being continued even now. Of the respondents, nearly 30 per cent stated that their families were influenced by the members to enter politics.

Table 3.11 : Maintaining Permanent Political Identity

Sl. No.	Category	No. of Respondents	Percentage
1.	Yes	376	94.00
2.	No	24	6.00
	Total	400	100.00

Source : Computed.

Orientation, mobilization and socialization of individuals and groups are resorted to for formation of an identity which will ultimately lead to action. People prefer identity as it is beneficial to them. In Tamil Nadu, political socialization and political mobilization were done at a massive level for the past four decades. Hence almost all the spaces are occupied by political functionaries leaving nothing to the general public. Of the four hundred respondents, 376 were positive towards identifying themselves with political organisations. Among the respondents one could observe a clear political commitment.

NOTES AND REFERENCES

1. Dennis Kavanagh, *Political Culture,* London: Macmillan, 1972, p. 28.
2. David O. Sears, "Political Socialization" in Greenstain and Polsby (eds.) *Handbook of Political Science: Micro Political Theory,* Vol.2, Sydney: Addison Wesley Publishing Company, 1975, p. 94.
3. A series of efforts were taken by the DMK party to orient the people in Dravidian ideology. Of them two are noteworthy, namely letters written to party members by C.N. Annadurai and M. Karunanidhi. C.N. Annadurai, *Thambikku Annavin Kadithangal* (in Tamil) (Letters of Annadurai) Chennai: Paari Nilayam, 1963, *Kalaignar Kaditham,* Chennai: Abirami Nilayam, 1986.
4. Andre Beteille, "Caste in Contemporary India," in *Caste Today* (ed.) C.J. Fuller, New Delhi, Oxford University Press, 1997.
5. Since the family structure in India is authoritarian in nature formation of opinion is so easy. S.C. Dube, *Modernization and Development: The Search for Alternative Paradigms,* New Delhi: Vistaar Publications, 1988, p.87.
6. G. Palanithurai, "Indian Politics from the Perspective of Tamil Nadu Polity," *The Indian Journal of Public Affairs and Policy Research,* Vols. 1&2: No. 1-4 (Jan.-Dec., 2000).
7. For more details see G. Palanithurai, "Communication and Mobilization of Ethnic Movement in Tamil Society," in *Ethnic Movement in India: Theory and Practice* (ed.) G. Palanithurai, New Delhi: Kanishka Publishers and Distributors. 1993, pp. 94-114.
8. R.L. Hardgrave, Jr. *The Dravidian Movement,* Bombay: Popular Prakashan, 1965.

4

POLITICAL PARTICIPATION

Political participation refers to individuals' involvement in activities which are related to the functioning of the political system. Political participation is a term having many meanings. It is applied to the activity of ordinary citizens and the leaders of political parties. Their activities are connected with the functioning of the political system. The activities range from voting, campaign, contributions and participating in marches to subjecting themselves to imprisonment for the cause of the party[1]. It is all centred round political activity. Activities are of different kinds. Some are covert in nature and some are overt in nature. Anyhow they are to be identified. Political activities are to be carried out by the individual and through institutions and organisations and the implications of the political activities could be seen through the nature and content of the decisions of the political institutions. Under the rubric of political behaviour, an array of books and articles have been written covering various aspects of political participation. Political scientists have developed a variety of methodological nuances to study political participation and they have fixed indicators to study the concept of participation. The indicators may vary from society to society[2]. To study political participation, researchers have developed a political activity index[3]. To measure the intensity of participation, they have assigned scores also. For this study in the Indian context we have to identify the channels through which activities are being carried out. They include identification of individuals with political organisation, interacting with others on political matters with a view to influencing others, participating in party meetings and conferences, taking up activities in the party, machinery participating in the electioneering activities of the party, contributing money for the party, participating in the activities of the party to exert pressure on the government, and enrolling members for the party.

In this study political participation is being studied with an index — a participation index exclusively developed for this work. It includes the political affiliation of the individuals, experience the individuals have gained in the party organisations, sense of political commitment based on the reasons for which the individuals identified themselves with political organisation, placement of the individuals in the organisations, explicit participation in the activities of the parties, kinds of activities in which individuals participated, influencing the family towards political participation, level of participation in the political activities of the party organisations, and experience in undergoing imprisonment for party activities. These indicators have been used to assess how far the respondents have participated in the political activities of the parties. The results are explained hereunder.

Table 4.1 : Party Affiliation

Sl. No.	Category	No. of Respondents	Percentage
1.	DK	41	10.25
2.	DMK	133	33.25
3.	AIADMK	96	24.00
4.	MDMK	40	10.00
5.	MGRADMK	27	6.75
6.	TMC	63	15.75
	Total	400	100.00

Source : Computed.

In determining the loyalty of an individual towards the nation and the ethnic group, people's affiliation to political parties matters much[4]. In Tamil Nadu so far two traditions have been witnessed, namely, national tradition and regional or ethnic tradition. Of the respondents, as Table 4.1 shows, nearly 85 per cent belong to the ethnic tradition. They belong to either DMK or AIADMK or MDMK or MGRADMK; 15 per cent of the respondents belong to Tamil Maanila Congress. Tamil Maanila Congress, though a regional political party, cherishes only national values and it always aligns with its parent organisation, namely Congress-I. The respondents have affiliated themselves with several organisations. These political organisations have their affinity with their province, language and culture. The respondents have thus got an identity political in nature. This ethnic tradition has greatly influenced their political participation, especially in election[5].

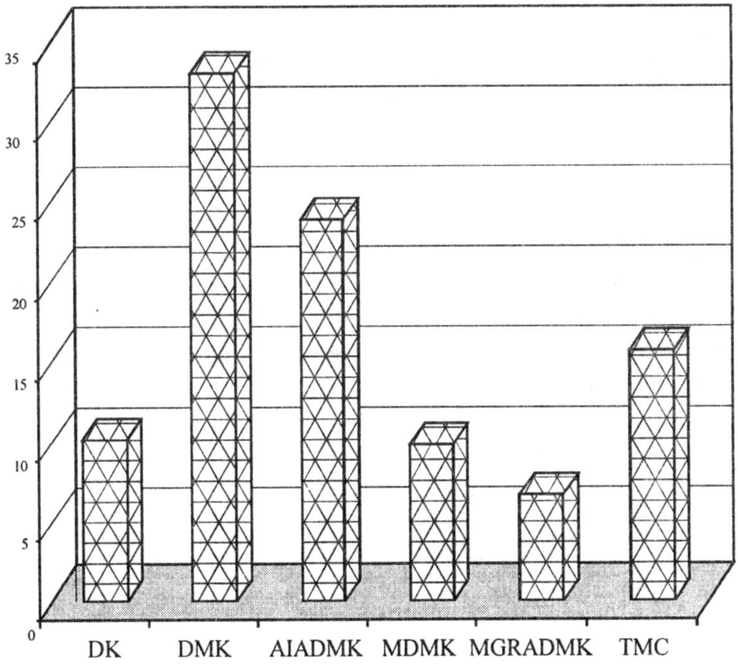

Fig. 4.1 : Party Affiliation

Table 4.2 : Political Experience

Sl. No.	Category	No. of Respondents	Percentage
1.	Before 1947	10	2.50
2.	1947 - 1956	27	6.75
3.	1957 - 1966	42	10.50
4.	1967 - 1976	103	25.75
5.	1977 - 1986	148	37.00
6.	1987 - 1996	70	17.50
7.	1997 & After	—	— .
	Total	400	100.00

Source : Computed.

The longevity of the political identity of the people is largely determined by the standing of the individuals in the respective organisations. For about two decades the ethnic political organisations oriented their members on ethnic issues. Hence, those who joined the organisation between 1950 and 1967 had a strong belief and conviction on the issues of the Tamils, namely, Tamil culture and Tamil language[6]. After they captured power, the intensity of mobilization on these aspects started declining. It is natural that the members who joined the same ethnic political parties after 1967 do not have such fervour for ethnic issues as they were not oriented in such ideology. As per Table 4.2 shows, 20 per cent of the respondents joined the parties before 1967. The remaining 80 per cent joined only at a later date. Reasonably one would expect a lift in the approach of the members towards ethnic issues.

Table 4.3 : Reasons for Choosing the Party

Sl. No.	Category	No. of Respondents	Percentage
1.	Ideology	93	23.25
2.	Leader Attraction	277	69.25
3.	Others	30	7.50
	Total	400	100.00

Source : Computed.

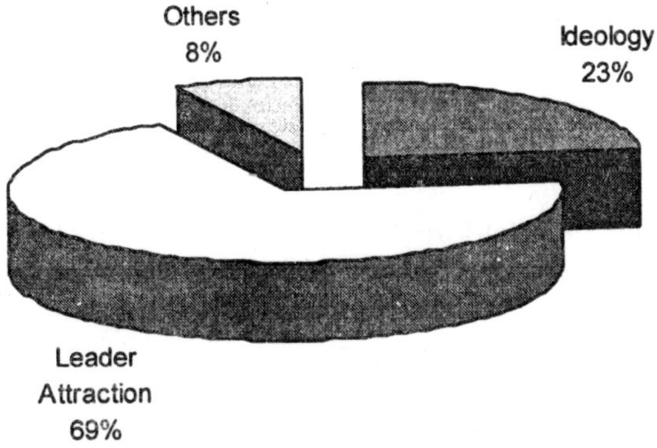

Fig 4.2 : Reasons for Choosing the Party

Throughout the world people exhibit their loyalty towards ethnic political organisations on the basis of their orientation towards the ethnic issues. Their continuation in the party and organisation is determined largely on the basis of the gains they have received and the ideological orientation they have had contextually and continuously. It is peculiar to Tamil Nadu that the people are more loyal to the leaders than the organisations. That is why the leaders can break the organisation very easily with their followers. Near about 69 per cent of the respondents replied that they are in the organisation not because of the ideology of the party. They are drawn and attracted towards the party because of the charismatic leadership of the party. This kind of loyalty towards the leaders make them give a go-by to the ideology and project themselves as factors.

Table 4.4 : Motivating Factors to Join Politics

Sl. No.	Category	No. of Respondents	Percentage
1.	Parents	10	2.50
2.	Friends	71	17.75
3.	Party Leaders	319	79.75
	Total	400	100.00

Source : Computed.

Political recruitment is a vital area of study in the domain of political behaviour. How people are drawn and how they are inducted and oriented towards organisation and ideology would determine the stability of the individual in the political organisation. According to Table 4.4, 80 per cent of the respondents unequivocally informed that they were drawn towards politics only by the leaders. The leaders speeches, writings and other activities attracted the people. As long as leaders are the factors for enlisting and enrolling a large number of members in the organisations, the same leaders are responsible for splits also. Attachment to the leaders is far greater than attachment to ideology. The ethnic political party leaders had several strategies to attract the masses. By adopting various strategies, they have highlighted ethnic issues. The ethnic issues were highlighted by the leaders in a convincing way and thereby the leaders gained popularity among the people.[7]

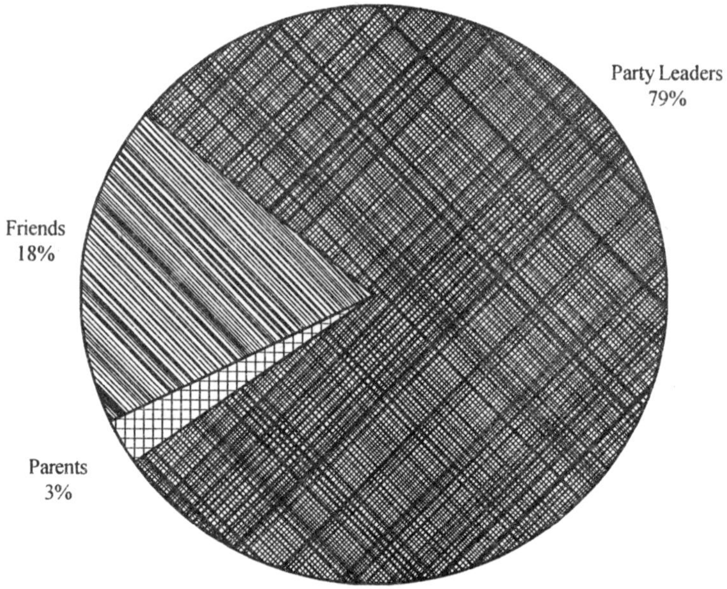

Fig. 4.3 : Motivating Factors to Join Politics

Table 4.5 : Position in Party

Sl. No.	Category	No. of Respondents	Percentage
1.	Mere Member	101	25.25
2.	Activist	177	44.25
3.	Leader	93	23.25
4.	Other	29	7.25
	Total	400	100.00

Source : Computed.

While identifying the member's loyalty towards the organisation, it is necessary to study the intensity of their attachment towards the organisation for proper evolution of the influence of these organisations in the process of the political system. According to Table 4.5, 7.25 per cent of the respondents are highly committed loyalists of the political organisations, while 25 per cent are mere members of the political organsiations. These 93 per cent of the respondents are oriented towards the party and the ideology, but vary considerably in their conceptions about politics and government[8]. In this case the respondents have a clear belief about the political system and the government. On the whole the respondents have a clear orientation, identity commitment and loyalty towards political organisations.

Table 4.6 : Participation in Party Activities

Sl. No.	Category	No. of Respondents	Percentage
1.	Yes	321	80.25
2.	No	79	19.75
	Total	400	100.00

Source : Computed.

The ideological orientation of the people and their loyalty to organisations can be assessed through their political activities. Activities are of different kinds. From participating in meetings to joining in protest marches, a variety of activities could be carried out by the individuals. Political involvement has its own hierarchy and it starts from spectator activities to gladiatorial activities. This hierarchy of political involvement varies from society to society. Generally no political activity could be considered normal or routine for everyday existence. Persons turn to politics only when their basic physical needs are met[9]. But in India the position is the reverse. Respondents have replied that they have actively participated in the party activities. Attending party meetings, organising party meetings, meeting local party leaders for party activities, participating in protest marches of the party, canvassing for party candidates in the elections, participating in the party elections and taking part in the celebrations of the party are the activities indicated by the respondents. The details are given in Table 4.7. Respondents have a wide choice to participate in the political activities of the organisations. The intensity of their commitment to party organisations is assessed on the basis of the nature of the activities in which they participate respectively[10].

Table 4.7 : Respondents' Involvement in Activities

Sl. No.	Category	No. of Respondents	Percentage
1.	Attending party meetings	86	26.79
2.	Organising party meetings	63	19.63
3.	Meeting local party leaders	92	28.66
4.	Participating in party protest marches	97	30.22
5.	Canvassing for party candidates in the election	96	29.91
6.	General election activities	72	22.43
7.	Participating in party conference	76	23.68
8.	Participating in party celebrations	81	25.23
9.	Participating in party elections	52	16.20
	Total	N = 321	100.00

Source : Computed.

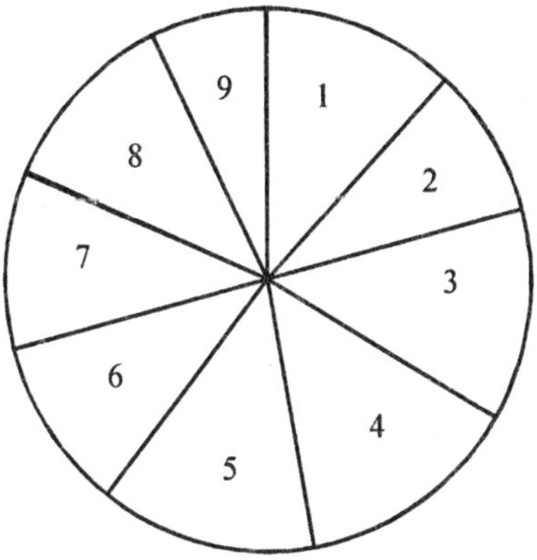

1. Attending Party Meetings 26.79%
2. Organising Party Meetings 19.63%
3. Meeting Local Party Leaders 28.66%
4. Participating in Party Protest Marches 30.22%
5. Canvassing for Party Candidates in the Election 29.91%
6. General Election Activities 22.43%
7. Participating in Party Conference 23.68%
8. Participating in Party Celebrations 25.23%
9. Participating in Party Election 16.2%

Fig. 4.4 : Respondents' Involvement in Political Activities

Generally political activities of the individuals are gauged by a number of ways, of which the number of family members involved in party politics is important. In some families there may not be more than one but in other families a few members may have political affiliation. According to Table 4.8, 70 per cent of the respondents said that excepting the respondent, other family members are not members of any political organisation, while 30 per cent said that their family members are active in politics. Hence, only one-third of the respondents have family commitment towards political organisations. Normally family and peer group have their own influence on the political activities of the individuals[11].

Table 4.8 : Family Membership in Political Party

Sl. No.	Category	No. of Respondents	Percentage
1.	Yes	117	29.25
2.	No	283	70.75
	Total	400	100.00

Source : Computed.

Participation has to be seen in terms of intensity: to what extent the individuals are committed towards the party, its ideology and its leaders. Individuals participate in different kinds of activities. But the question is whether their participation is occasional or regular. Near about 70 per cent of the representatives stated that they are very active during elections, evincing keen interest and participating in all the activities. So the activeness of the individuals has been reduced to the party's election activities. Table 4.9 shows the level of involvement of the respondents in political activities. It is an irony in Indian democracy that election is considered a major activity or even the prime activity in democracy and hence all have given importance to election. As for all the other activities, people do not show as keen an interest as they evince in electoral politics. It would appear as though the member's loyalty is being tested only during the time of election.

Table 4.9 : Level of Involvement in Political Activities

Sl. No.	Nature of Occasion	Rarely	Occasionally	Frequently	Total
1.	General Elections	—	116 (29.00)	284 (71.00)	400 (100)
2.	Party Elections	7 (1.75)	204 (51.00)	189 (47.25)	400 (100)
3.	Conference	18 (4.50)	212 (53.00)	170 (42.50)	400 (100)
4.	Party Protest Activities	11 (2.75)	263 (65.75)	126 (31.50)	400 (100)

Source : Computed.

There is yet another indicator, namely, the mode of sacrifice of the members for the party or organisation. Imprisonment for a general cause is considered the most intensive mode of participation in political activities. In Tamil Nadu it has been the practice to defy the order of the government and undergo imprisonment for a general cause by the committed members of the party. They are subsequently honoured by the party. Of the respondents, 71 per cent had the experience of undergoing imprisonment. They are highly committed to the parties. On two occasions they were imprisoned. During the time of the anti-Hindi agitation and at the time of outbreak of ethnic violence in Sri Lanka. Ethnic loyalty is shown during crises. During the anti-Hindi agitation people wanted to show their solidarity towards the political organisation in safeguard in the interests of Tamil language. Equally they exhibited their identity towards their ethnic group when Sri Lankan Tamils faced a crisis in Sri Lanka in the year 1983.

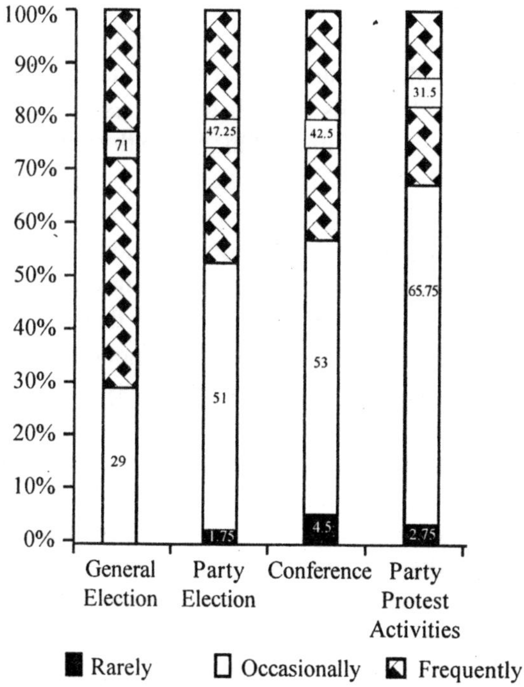

Fig. 4.5 : Level of Involvement in Political Activities

Table 4.10 : Resource Support to Party Activities

Sl. No.	Category	No. of Respondents	Percentage
1.	Yes	287	71.75
2.	No	113	28.25
	Total	400	100.00

Source : Computed.

Yet, another indicator of participation, namely, the contribution of resources to the party, has to be taken into cognisance. Donating resources periodically to the party and political activities of the party forms a key indicator in determining the intensity of participation and commitment towards the party[12]. Monetary contributions to parties and activities of political parties has been discussed and analysed elaborately against the backdrop of ethical standards. About 67 per cent of the respondents contributed liberally to their parties. The political parties have started a practice of collecting donations from the people and subscription from the members for the organisations with the aim of creating a sense of commitment on the part of the individuals towards the parties.

Next to the contribution of money to the party, sticking on to the party continuously is also considered a factor for the anchorage of the party in the society. Ethnic political parties have witnessed splits many times and on all those occasions a large number of members were expected to cross over to the new outfits since people are oriented towards the party leaders rather than the party ideology. As Table 4.11 shows, 71 per cent of the respondents have expressed that they have not so far changed their loyalty; 29 per cent said that they have moved over to the new organisations; and 29 per cent are oriented towards the party leaders rather than the ideology. While analysing the responses of the respondents one can find the real reasons for the change of loyalty: 50 per cent of respondents informed that they are attracted towards the leaders, while 19 per cent replied that they are drawn towards the party due to the ideology. Around 23 per cent of the respondents said that they are moving from one party to another due to the corrupt practices adopted by the parent organisation. After analysing the reasons for change of loyalty, one would be tempted to ask how often they change loyalty: 64 per cent of the respondents said that they have changed their loyalty once in their life, while 26 per cent replied that they have changed their loyalty twice in their life. People have been propelled to move from one ethnic political party to another since the conflict and division are not on the basis of ideology but on the basis of the personal feuds of the leaders. Thus people are oriented towards the leadership rather than the ideology.

Table 4.11 : Change of Party Loyalty

Sl. No.	Category	No. of Respondents	Percentage
1.	Yes	116	29.00
2.	No	284	71.00
	Total	400	100.00

Source : Computed.

Table 4.12 : Reasons for Change

Sl. No.	Category	No. of Respondents	Percentage
1.	Leaders' attraction	58	50.00
2.	Corruption	27	23.27
3.	Ideology	23	19.83
4.	Compulsion	8	6.90
	Total	116	100.00

Source : Computed.

Table 4.13 : Number of Times Party Loyalty Changed

Sl. No.	Category	No. of Respondents	Percentage
1.	One	75	64.66
2.	Two	31	26.72
3.	Three	10	8.62
	Total	116	100.00

Source : Computed.

NOTES AND REFERENCES

1. Sidney Verba, Norman H. Nie and Jae-on Kim, *A Seven-nation Comparison: Participation and Political Equality,* Cambridge: Cambridge University Press, 1978, p. 46.
2. Jae-on Kim, Norman H. Nie and Sidney Verba, "The Amount and Concentration of Political Activity," *Political Methodology* 1 (Spring, 1974) 105-132.
3. Sidney Verba, Norman H. Nie, and Jae-on Kim, *The Modes of Democratic Participation : A Cross National Analysis*, Beverly Hills California: Sage Professional Papers in Comparative Politics, 1971.

   Sidney Verba, Norman H. Nie, Ana Barbic, Galen Irwin, Henk Molleman and Goldie Shabad, "The Modes of Participation: Continuities in Research", *Comparative Political Studies* 6 (1973), pp. 235-250.
4. Gerald Curtis, *Election Campaigning Japanese Style,* New York: Columbia University Press, 1971.
5. Narendra Subramanian, *Ethnicity and Populist Mobilization,* New Delhi: Oxford University Press, 1999, p. 171.
6. Nambi Aarooran, *Tamil Renaissance and Dravidian Nationalism 1916-1944,* Madurai : Koodal Publishers, 1980.
7. G. Palanithurai, *Political Communications and Political Mobilization : A Study in Dravidian Movement,* Annamalai Nagar: Department of Political Science, 1989.
8. Lester W. Milbrath, *Political Participation,* Chicago : Rand McNally & Company, 1965, p. 64.
9. James David, *Human Nature in Politics,* New York: Wiley, 1963, Chapter I &II .
10. Sidney Verba, Norman H. Nie, *Participation in America: Political Democracy and Social Equality,* New York : Harper & Row Publishers, 1972.
11. Angus Campbell, "Surge and Decline : A Study of Electoral Change", *Public Opinion Quarterly,* XXIV (1960 Fall).

5

ETHNIC IDENTITY

People normally would lead a community life with the objective of fulfilling their common needs. They organise themselves as groups and distinguish themselves from others. Sometimes they would be differentiated by others. This process of identifying themselves with groups, symbols and territories is called identity formation. Scholars in ethnicity define ethnic groups in terms of objective attributes with reference to subjective feelings and in relation to behaviour. There must be some distinguishing factors or features that clearly separate one group of people from another. The subjective definition is that a group people arrive at subjective self-consciousness. Behavioural definitions are really a form of objective definition since they assume that there are specific concrete ways in which ethnic groups behave or do not behave particularly in relation to and in interaction with other groups[1]. Thus ethnicity is a sense of ethnic identity which has been defined by De Vos as consisting of the subjective symbolic or emblematic use by a group of people...of any aspect of culture, in order to differentiate themselves from other groups[2]. In the recent past there have been two major identities which have drawn the attention of academics to ponder over the identification of the people either towards ethnicity or towards nations. They are ethnic identity and national identity. Generally national identity means the process of identifying the people with the nation[3]. There has been a confusion over the concepts of nationalism and patriotism. Generally nationalism refers to the identification of people with the nation and patriotism refers to the identification of people with the Nation-State. For a long period, ethnic identity was considered a negative factor for nation building process. At present the same ethnic identity has been defined as national identity. Moreover, the identity of individuals tends to vary from context to context. In this work ethnic identity refers to the identification of the people with language, culture and other ethnic symbols.

To assess the identity of the individuals with ethnicity a battery of questions related to ethnic aspects was formulated and they were administered to the respondents. Explanations were also sought for their identity and loyalty. Language and culture are the two factors which determine the identity formation of ethnic groups. Therefore, questions have been included on language and culture. Starting from their primordial sentiments, people have several identities and yet they prefer to stick on the one identity for a long period. In Tamil Nadu, though the people perpetuate ethnic identity, their sentiments are with caste organisations also. Equally their sentiments are with the nation also. Identity of individuals is assessed on the basis of their perceived actions on the symbols of ethnicity or nation or caste or any other symbols which they cherish. One cannot assume that people have only a single identity. They may have different identities but the intensity may vary from symbol to symbol. Anchorage and longevity of identity can be determined by a variety of factors. A nationalist can be a patriot and equally he may be a regionalist. How people identify themselves with their group or caste or region or language or culture is described and explained hereunder.

Table 5.1 : Attachment of Language and Caste

Sl. No.	Category	Yes	No	Total
1.	Identification with Caste	197 (49.25)	203 (50.75)	400 (100)
2.	Special Liking for Language	367 (91.75)	33 (8.25)	400 (100)
3.	Equating Mother-Tongue with Mother	353 (88.25)	47 (11.75)	400 (100)
4.	Aware of Tamil Thai Vazhthu	283 (70.75)	117 (29.25)	400 (100)

Source : Computed.

Of the respondents, nearly 49 per cent are having affiliation with caste organisations. At the same time they maintain membership or ethnic political party; 91 per cent expressed their special liking for their mother-tongue Tamil; 88 per cent of the respondents equated the mother-tongue with mother. In Tamil Nadu, a song praising the language—Tamil—is to be sung in every public function. Hence, almost all the members of the ethnic movement would be aware of it. As per Table 5.1, 70 per cent of the respondents have awareness about the song. Theoretically language has been used as a factor to bring about unity among the people to form a group and it is a symbol which can be used to exite the emotions and sentiments of the people[4]. In Tamil Nadu language has played a major role in shaping ethnic politics[5]. Equally Tamil culture performs a key role in shaping the thought of the Tamils in the political process of the province[6].

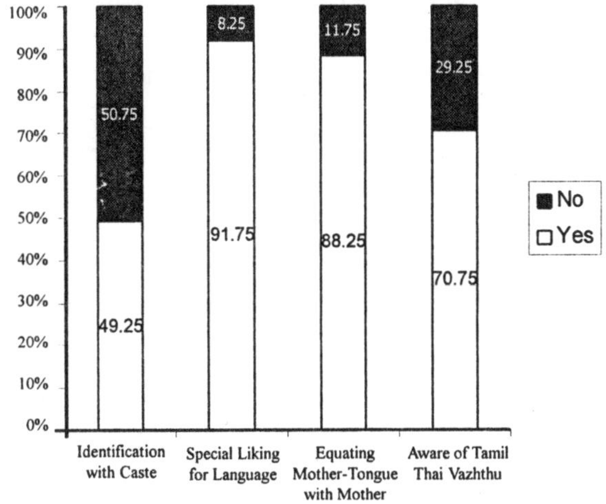

Fig. 5.1 : Attachment to Language and Caste

Table 5.2 : Following Tamil Calendar

Sl. No.	Category	No. of Respondents	Percentage
1.	Yes	127	31.75
2.	No	273	68.25
	Total	400	100.00

Source : Computed.

While the Tamils are attached to the Tamil language, it is necessary to consider whether they follow it in their life. Following the Tamil calendar, sending their wards to Tamil medium schools, celebrating Tamil festivals are some of the symbols. All the activities of the individuals are according to the English calendar. Their activities are globalised. Even though they have faith in their language, culture and calendar, they follow only the English calendar. But around 31 per cent of the respondents said that they follow the Tamil calendar. Following the English calendar has not been considered as contradicting their loyalty towards their own language and culture. Their aversion and antagonism are reserved for only Hindi. Both English and Hindi are foreign languages to the Tamils. Yet people regard Hindi as dominant and alien to Tamil society. This is a kind of contradiction one would find not only in Tamil ethnicity but also in many of the societies[7].

Table 5.3 : Reasons for not Following Tamil Calendar

Sl. No.	Category	No. of Respondents	Percentage
1.	Unsuited to routine life	197	72.16
2.	Do not have interest	76	27.84
	Total	*N*=273	100.00

Source : Computed.

The respondents explained that they follow only the English calendar because they are functionally linked with the English calendar.

Yet another symbol is celebrating a Tamil culture festival in Tamil Nadu. "Pongal" as a popular Tamil festival celebrated by all in Tamil Nadu. Deepavali was considered as a Hindu festival before the launching of the Dravidian Movement. Of the festivals, Pongal is considered a festival of the Tamils. Awareness was created among the Tamils about the importance of Tamil festivals and so the members who committed themselves to ethnic organisations followed the instructions of the ethnic parties and celebrated the festivals with gaiety.

Table 5.4 : Giving Importance to Pongal Celebration

Sl. No.	Category	No. of Respondents	Percentage
1.	Yes	239	59.75
2.	No	161	40.25
	Total	400	100.00

Source : Computed.

Table 5.5 : Reason for Importance to Pongal Celebration

Sl. No.	Category	No. of Respondents	Percentage
1.	Tamil Festival	101	62.73
2.	Farmers' Festival	28	17.39
3.	Harvesting Festival	32	19.88
	Total	*N*=161	100.00

Source : Computed.

About 53 per cent of the respondents said that they did not celebrate the Hindu rituals and ceremonies; 46 per cent said that they celebrate Hindu festivals; 59 per cent of the respondents replied that they celebrate only the Tamil festivals. The respondents has given importance to Pongal festival as it is a festival of Tamils, farmers and harvest. The kind of transformation is not an accident. It is the outcome of the conscious efforts of the ethnic organisations and their leaders to change the consciousness of the people. This process has been termed as, symbolic ethnicity[8]. It is a love for the past and it is characterised by a nostalgic allegiance to the culture of the group or community. It is nothing but taking pride in the tradition, history, culture and language of the group and persuading people to a state of mind marked by a sincere desire to return to the past. All the cultural patterns which are transformed into symbols are themselves guided by a common pragmatic imperative and they must be visible and clear in meaning to large numbers of people of different generations. In Tamil Nadu efforts were made consciously by the ethnic organisations towards this end[9].

When they give importance to Tamil language and Tamil culture, it is a pertinent question whether they give the same importance to educating their children in mother-tongue : 40 per cent of the respondents replied that they are sending their wards to English medium schools as they get wider opportunity at a later stage for their livelihood and prosperity; but 60 per cent of the respondents said that they are sending their wards only to Tamil medium schools. This does not indicate any sense of loyalty and commitment towards the Tamil language. Since English medium schools are costlier, they prefer Tamil schools. They have different reasons for this decision. By putting their wards in English medium schools, their wards can get job opportunity anywhere. Only some of the respondents said that they preferred Tamil medium schools because of the importance attached to the language. People have developed an aversion towards Hindi and not towards English. They felt that English would provide more opportunity for their wards in employment.

Table 5.6 : Sending the Children to English Medium School

Sl. No.	Category	No. of Respondents	Percentage
1.	Yes	161	40.25
2.	No	239	59.75
	Total	400	100.00

Source : Computed.

Table 5.7 : Reason for not Sending Children to English Medium Schools

Sl. No.	Category	No. of Respondents	Percentage
1.	Importance to mother-tongue	129	53.98
2.	Standard of education	33	13.81
3.	Poor economic condition	17	7.11
4.	School not available in village	42	17.57
5.	Do not have interest	18	7.53
	Total	*N*=239	100.00

Source : Computed.

From the response of the respondents as shown in Table 5.8, one would come to the conclusion that, in the Tamil mind, Hindi is associated with a social movement[10]. Seventy-five per cent of the respondents categorically informed that they prefer only English at the national level, while only 24 per cent preferred Hindi. People have reasons to take positions. Those who prefer Hindi argued that Tamils can establish their sway in many pockets of this country. It can only help Tamils. Tamils have tremendous potentiality and capacity and their potentiality could be used productively. Those who reject the above argument offer an array of explanations as per Table 5.9: 9 per cent said that Hindi is only a language of a few states and so cannot be accepted nationally; 33 per cent argued that English opens up wider opportunity throughout the world and hence it can be accepted; 7 per cent felt that Hindi will effect the growth of the Tamil language; 30 per cent argued that they cannot bear the load of three languages; 19 per cent said that they had faith in their mother-tongue. As per Table 5.10, 82 per cent of the respondents preferred that Tamil should be declared a national classical language. Though they have different explanations for the language issue, they are one in this respect. Here one can understand the respondents' faith in the language. This faith had been created by the sustained efforts of the ethnic movement in Tamil Nadu[11].

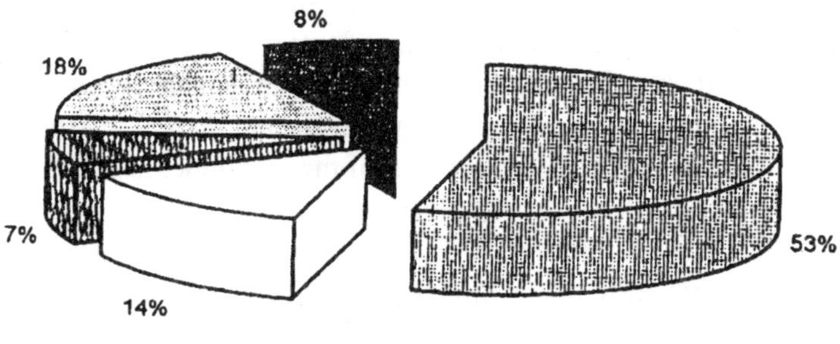

Fig. 5.2 : Reason for not sending Children to English Medium Schools

In order to identify whether the respondents have any hardline ideas on the rights of the ethnic group, a battery of questions were asked, to which categorical answer were given. One question thus asked was whether land ownership should be reserved only for Tamilians in Tamil Nadu, since most of the radical Tamil movements in Tamil Nadu put forth the argument that the Tamil economy is under the control of the people coming from other states and lands have been grabbed by the moneyed groups migrating from North India. As Table 5.11 shows, 77 per cent of the respondents rejected this idea but 23 per cent replied that it can be done as it has been in Kashmir. Asked whether employment opportunity in Tamil Nadu should be given only to Tamils, 46 per cent of the respondents rejected the idea and stated that if this approach is followed, opportunities for Tamils in other states would be closed, but 54 per cent said that opportunities should be given only to Tamil as Tamil Nadu can generate adequate employment opportunity to meet only the requirements of Tamils. Since Tamil Nadu has effectively operationalised the population policy, Tamil Nadu need not depend on other states for employment opportunity. There is yet another argument, namely, that "be Indian and buy Indian" can be adapted to "be Tamilian and buy Tamilian". Around 53 per cent of the respondents said that if this policy is followed the Tamils could save their enterprises in global competition.

Love for Tamils can be promoted and local products can be supported, but 47 per cent of the respondents rejected the idea saying that the products of Tamils cannot then be sold outside Tamil Nadu. For another important questions whether the medium of instruction in schools can be Tamil, 78 per cent of the respondents said that it can be only Tamil, by which alone knowledge could be acquired very effectively. As for the CBSE schools and the Navodaya Schools some felt that they are a hindrance to Tamil medium schools. However, 77 per cent of the respondents said that these schools can also function and the students/parents should have the freedom to choose. "Opportunity should not be denied" is the opinion of these respondents.

Table 5.8 : Respondents' Acceptance of Language at National Level

Sl. No.	Category	No. of Respondents	Percentage
1.	English	303	75.75
2.	Hindi	97	24.25
	Total	400	100.00

Source : Computed.

Table 5.9 : Reason for not Accepting Hindi

Sl. No.	Category	No. of Respondents	Percentage
1.	Language of only some states	28	9.24
2.	English is a common language	100	33.01
3.	Hindi will affect Tamil language	23	7.59
4.	Cannot study three languages	93	30.69
5.	Tamil faith	59	19.47
	Total	*N*=303	100.00

Source : Computed.

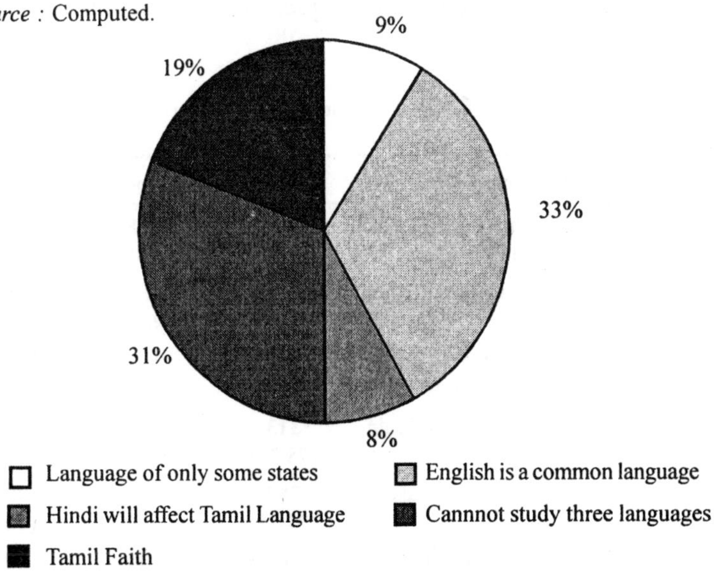

Fig. 5.3 : Reason for not Accepting Hindi

Table 5.10 : Respondents' View on Tamil as National Classical Language

Sl. No.	Category	No. of Respondents	Percentage
1.	Yes	331	82.75
2.	No	69	17.25
	Total	400	100.00

Source : Computed.

In order to bring about Tamil consciousness among Tamils, every aspect of life should be oriented towards Tamil. As per Table 5.11, 71 per cent of the respondents strongly felt that in every aspect Tamil should be used. Then only Tamils can have the feeling that they have a status.

An interesting question was put to the respondents: Who is a Tamil? As per Table 5.12, 45 per cent of the respondents replied that those who speak Tamil as mother-tongue except Brahmins are Tamils, while 35 per cent said that those who work for Tamil welfare can be considered Tamils. People are not clear in their approach and definition. Not only the people, even politicians have this confusion.

Table 5.11 : Respondents' Love for Tamil and Tamilians

Sl. No.	Category	Agree	Disagree	Total
1.	Landownership only for Tamils in Tamil Nadu	92 (23.00)	308 (77.00)	400 (100)
2.	Employment opportunity only for Tamils	216 (54.00)	184 (46.00)	400 (100)
3.	Tamil people must purchase only from Tamil shops	211 (52.75)	189 (47.25)	400 (100)
4.	Medium of education should be Tamil	313 (78.25)	87 (21.75)	400 (100)
5.	Tamil to be used in all aspects	287 (71.75)	113 (28.25)	400 (100)
6.	Tamil identity is affected by CBSE & Navodaya schools	92 (23.00)	308 (77.00)	400 (100)

Source : Computed.

Table 5.12 : Respondents' Opinion about Who is a Tamilian

Sl. No.	Category	No. of Respondents	Percentage
1.	All Tamil speaking peoples (except Aryans)	183	45.75
2.	Born in Tamil Nadu	43	10.75
3.	Working for Tamil welfare	141	35.25
4.	Faith in Tamil Nadu	33	8.25
	Total	400	100.00

Source : Computed.

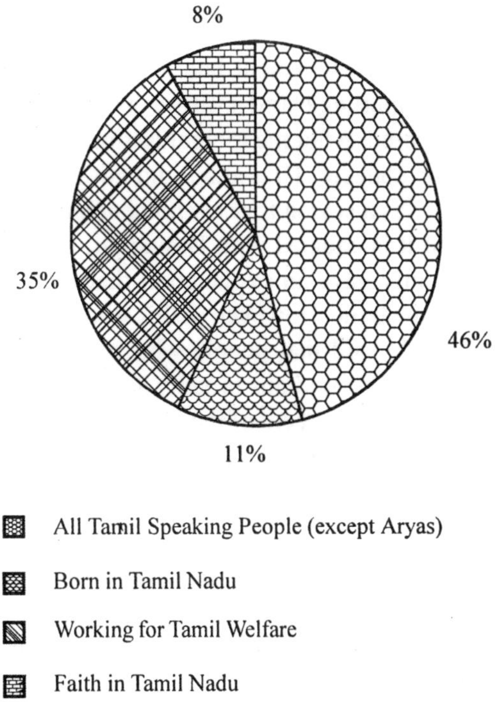

Fig. 5.4 : Respondents' Opinion about who is a Tamilian

Table 5.13 : Respondents' Opinion about Reported Differences between Dravidian and Tamilian

Sl. No.	Category	No. of Respondents	Percentage
1.	Tamil, Telugu, Malayalam, Kannada speaking people are Dravidians but only Tamil speaking peoples are Tamilians	204	51.00
2.	Dravidian by Race but Tamilian by Language	103	25.75
3.	Both are same	93	23.25
	Total	400	100.00

Source : Computed.

Since the Dravidian Movement had a strong social base it took roots only in language and culture as the intellectual background was prepared. After the reorganisation of states on the basis of language the concept 'Dravidian' did not get momentum and as a result there was a search for new nomenclature. Tamilian gained currency and it is equated with Dravidian. Leaders in the movement conveniently gave an explanation that Dravidian is a race but Tamilian is an ethnic. However, in this study 51 per cent of the respondents clearly said that people who speak Malayalam, Telugu and Kannada are Dravidians broadly and those who speak Tamil are Tamilians, 25.75 per cent of the respondents replied that Dravidian is a race and Tamilian is an ethnic; and 23 per cent of the respondents clarified that both are the same and there is no difference between the two.

Table 5.14 : Respondents' veiws on Who is an Indian

Sl. No.	Category	No. of Respondents	Percentage
1.	We are Indians	361	90.25
2.	Hindi speaking peoples'	39	9.75
	Total	400	100.00

Source : Computed.

Asked "who is an Indian?" 10 per cent of the respondents said that Hindi speaking people are Indians, but 90 per cent said that all those belong to the ethnic political parties and regional political parties are Indians. They closely identify with ethnic values. They exhibit their loyalty towards their mother-tongue. The same respondents say that they are Indians. They identify themselves with an ethnic group but at the same time they also identify themselves with the nation. This has been unfortunately considered a paradox[12]. People have many identities. But these identities do not thwart the loyalty of the citizens towards the nation. Projection the identities has many reasons. It does not mean that they are disloyal to the nation.

Table 5.15 : Respondents' Opinion on whether Development is Possible Using Tamil

Sl. No.	Category	No. of Respondents	Percentage
1.	Yes	363	90.75
2.	No	37	9.25
	Total	400	100.00

Source : Computed.

The Tamil's love of Tamil is not mere emotional attachment to the mother-tongue, but something more. They sincerely believe that, by following the mother-tongue development can be achieved. People say that science, technology and medicine can be used effectively if all transactions are carried out in the people's language. When Tamil is used as a language for all transactions in government offices and educational institutions, there will not be any barrier between the people and the government. For the development of Tamil society, it is perceived that Tamil language is essential.

Table 5.16 : Approval of Usage of Concept of Dravida

Sl. No.	Category	No. of Respondents	Percentage
1.	Yes	186	46.50
2.	No	214	53.50
	Total	400	100.00

Source : Computed.

There are two concepts used interchangeably in Tamil Nadu, namely, Dravida with Tamils. Adequate explanations are available to equate Dravida with Tamils. Yet there are distinctions as perceived by the people of this province. As per Table 5.15, 53 per cent of the respondents argued that Dravida cannot be equated with Tamils as the Tamils are only one of the sub-groups constituted in the Dravidian community. They have logical reasons to accept Tamils as a distinct concept popularised after 1956 in Tamil Nadu. About 47 per cent of the respondents believed that both concepts are same and that is why even today parties are using this concept as a prefix for the name of the political parties in Tamil Nadu.

Table 5.17 : Reasons for Tamilization Taking Place

Sl. No.	Category	No. of Respondents	Percentage
1.	Dravidian by Race but Tamilian by Language	39	20.97
2.	After the separation of State Tamil Nadu called Dravida Nadu (main reason is to avoid Aryans)	147	79.03
	Total	*N*=186	100.00

Source : Computed.

Respondents of the study maintain that by nationality they are Indians, by race they Dravidian, and, by language they are Tamils. Seventy-nine per cent state that they want to distinguish themselves from the Brahmins and hence they want to have an identity of their own. They tried their best to galvanise the support of all non-Brahmins under the term Dravida, including Kannadika, Andhraites, Keralites and Tamils but they could not succeed. Hence they concentrated switched on Tamils. "Dravida" was sought to be popularised in Madras Presidency but it was not popular after 1956, because the states were organised on the basis of language.

Table 5.18 : Contradiction between the Dravidian Movement and Parties

Sl. No.	Category	No. of Respondents	Percentage
1.	Yes	357	89.25
2.	No	43	10.75
	Total	400	100.00

Source : Computed.

Political parties were organised on ethnic lines to highlight the issues of the Tamils for achieving development for them. But, in the course of years, these political parties had to change many of the aspects of their policies and programmes due to the circumstances as perceived by the people. As per Table 5.18, 89 per cent of the respondents felt that there is a contradiction between the basic objectives of the Dravidian Movement and the course of ethnic political parties of today. There is now a total contradiction between the activities of the ethnic political parties and the ethnic movement.

Primordial loyalty was utilised by the ethnic leaders to mobilise the people and tradition was the focal point for their mobilization. Arguments are now projected that ethnic political parties are relying more on Tamil tradition than on nationalism. This was denied by the respondents. Nearly 90 per cent of them said that Tamil nationalism never thrived on tradition. Tamil history has been repeatedly quoted only to highlight the rationality with which life was led by Tamils. It does not mean that Tamil nationalism moved on tradition. They further stated that Tamil nationalism followed only a scientific approach.

Table 5.19 : Respondents' Views on Tamil Nationalism and Tradition

Sl. No.	Category	No. of Respondents	Percentage
1.	Yes	39	9.75
2.	No	361	90.25
	Total	400	100.00

Source : Computed.

Table 5.20 : Dravidian Movement Used only Scientific Approach

Sl. No.	Category	No. of Respondents	Percentage
1.	Yes	361	90.75
2.	No	39	9.25
	Total	400	100.00

Source : Computed.

Table 5.21 : Effects of Anti-Hindi Agitation

Sl. No.	Category	No. of Respondents	Percentage
1.	All government Correspondence is in English	114	28.50
2.	Increased time for Tamil in Radio, Television programmes	70	17.50
3.	All the Central Government offices used English and Tamil	99	24.75
4.	Changed the name of Dalmiapuram	24	6.00
5.	Stopped all the activities of Hindi zealots in Tamil Nadu	93	23.25
	Total	400	100.00

Source : Computed.

Normally, social movements gain momentum only when the people of the movement see success in store for their activities. In the same way the Dravidian Movement gained currency among the people in Tamil Nadu. The anti-Hindi agitation was an historic event in the Tamil ethnic movement which brought about a change in the provincial government. The members of the movement sincerely felt that the anti-Hindi agitation created certain changes in the process of governance and the respondents listed them: 28.50 per cent of the respondents stated that all result of the anti-Hindi agitation, letters from the Central Government were only in English and not in Hindi; 17.50 per cent said that Doordarshan and All India Radio allotted more time for Tamil programmes; 24.75 per cent said that along with English, Tamil was used for correspondence between departments of the Central and the State governments.

Table 5.22 : Tamil Nadu is Neglected by the Centre

Sl. No.	Category	No. of Respondents	Percentage
1.	Yes	311	77.75
2.	No	89	22.25
	Total	400	100.00

Source : Computed.

When the Dravidian Movement was at its peak, people used to say that Tamil Nadu had been neglected by the federal government. They quoted frequently the issue of conversion of the metre gauge railway into broad gauge. Likewise they quoted industrialization. In industrialization, Tamil Nadu was prominent during the sixties[13]. The politicians of ethnic political parties used to criticise the Central Government for its failure to develop Tamil Nadu. They had yet another issue — the language issue which was clubbed with the development issue. Even now the members of ethnic political parties have the feeling that Tamil Nadu is being neglected. One can gauge the mood of the members of the ethnic political parties in the context of the development achieved in Tamil Nadu.

Table 5.23 : Faith in Ethnic Parties

Sl. No.	Category	No. of Respondents	Percentage
1.	Yes	297	74.25
2.	No	103	25.75
	Total	400	100.00

Source : Computed.

Most of the ethnic political parties were vociferous in articulating the demands of the Tamils. While doing this they used to attack all the national political parties and the federal government. Now the position of ethnic political parties has changed. They have started aligning with the national political parties for election and formation of government at the centre. The hardcore elements in the ethnic political parties have moved out and formed diehard organisations and adopted extremist courses of action. They openly demand separate Tamil Nadu for Tamils. It is believed that the ethnic political parties are supporting the activities of these extremist groups in Tamil Nadu. Hence a question on this was put to the respondents and 67 per cent of them said that it is true that the extremist groups are being supported by the ethnic political parties in Tamil Nadu. They extend approval to the activities of the extremist groups, for instance, by way of extending their support to LTTE in Sri Lanka.

Table 5.24 : Approval of Anti-Naitonal Activities of Ethnic Party Leaders

Sl. No.	Category	No. of Respondents	Percentage
1.	Yes	271	67.75
2.	No	129	32.25
	Total	400	100.00

Source : Computed.

It is inferred from the above analysis that the respondents wanted to have a separate identity and they will be happy to maintain the distinct identity. However, they are practical in their approach. It is not factors such as language or culture which determine their course of action but only economic advantage which determines the activities of the people. Efforts were made by ethnic political parties to create Tamil consciousness among the people but the people are rational in taking decisions. Whenever the ethnic identity is advantageous for them, they project their ethnic identity. But they are not dogmatic. They tend to change their approach whenever necessary. They have perceived the changes of approach of the ethnic political parties and acted in accordance with the changing circumstances. On most occasions one can find economic rationality in their perception.

Yet they keep up the ethnic identity, because they have been oriented for a long period on ethnic values.

NOTES AND REFERENCES

1. Paul R. Brass, "Ethnic Identity Formation," in *Ethnicity* (eds.) John Hutchinson and Anthony D. Smith, New York: Oxford University Press, 1996, p. 85.
2. George De Vos, "Ethnic Pluralism," in George De Vos and Lola Romanucci-Ross (eds.) *Ethnic Identity Cultural Continuities and Change,* California: May Field Publishing Company, 1975, p.16.
3. Walker Conner, "Beyond Reason: The Nature of the Ethnonational Bond". in *Ethnicity* (eds.) John Hutchinson and Anthony D. Smith, New York: Oxford University Press, 1996, p. 70.
4. Paul R. Brass, *Ethnicity and Nationalism: Theory and Comparison,* New Delhi: Sage Publications, 1991.
5. Nambi Aarooran, *Tamil Renaissance and Dravidian Nationalism 1905-1944,* Madurai: Koodal Publishers, 1980, E.F. Irsdrick. Tamil Revivalism in 1930's Chennai: Cre-A Publication, 1986.
6. M.R. Barnett, *The Politics of Cultural Nationalism in South India,* Princeton: Princeton University Press, 1976.
7. Foon, C.S., "On the Incompatibility of Ethnic and National Loyalties: Reframing the Issue," *Canadian Review of Studies in Nationalism,* 3 :1 (1986).
8. Herbert J. Gans, "Symbolic Ethnicity," in *Ethnicity* (eds.) John Hutchinson and Anthony D. Smith, New York: Oxford University Press, 1996, p. 146.
9. S.V. Shanmugam, *Mozhi Valarchiyum Mozhi Unarvuim (Tamil) (Language Development and Languge Feeling*), Madras : Manivasakar Pathipagam, 1989.
10. For more details about the language movement see E. Annamalai, *Language Movements in India,* Mysore : Central Institute of Indian Languages, 1979.
11. C.N. Annadurai, *Tamil Nadu Marumalarchi (Renaissance of the Tamils),* Madras : Parinilayam, 1975.
12. To understand the paradoxes in Dravidian Movement see, K. Sivathambi, *Understanding Dravidian Movement,* Madras: New Century Book House, 1986.
13. C.N. Annadurai, *Thambikku Annavin Kadithangal (Tamil) (Letters of C.N. Annadurai),* Vol. 12, Madras : Parinilayam, 1981.

6

NATIONAL LOYALTY

The concepts of nationalism Nation-State and nation-building are phenomena of the 19th century[1]. They were generated in Western Europe and gradually spread throughout the world. The same concept of nationalism was used differently in academic writings in the later half of the 20th century. Ethnicity is another concept which gained currency both in the west and east as it became a dominant factor in the political process of the Nation-States. To reconcile the two concepts of nationalism and ethnicity academics struggle in the midst of a plethora of concepts such as statism, national integration, state building, nation building, province building, nationalism, sub-nationalism, ethno-nationalism, regionalism, sub-regionalism, tribalism, casteism and collectivism. To study the concept of nationalism, a variety of approaches were developed[2]. Ever since the concept of Nation-State gained currency among the people and the academics, tendencies opposing the Nation-State were construed as anti-nation activities and so they were treated as illegal and unlawful activities. The feeling of identity with the Nation-State was perceived as nationalism. Thus nationalism is an affirmative action of the people towards the Nation-State. But, after the Second World War, the process of modernization and westernization made people of different regions, races, cultures, and languages realise their position and form an identity with their culture, race and language[3]. The perceived unevenness in terms of socio-economic and political benefits attained by different groups or collectivities concientised the people and thereby was created a new belief, faith and identity. A new nomenclature was coined for this new phenomenon which is now called ethnicity[4]. It has become a new exercise to formulate a sense of identity with a group of people on the basis of either language or culture or region or race[5].

This kind of new formations and formulations caused a host of changes in national and regional politics of many of the countries of the world[6]. Many of the developed countries have taken note of the change in the perception of the people about the politics of development and acted in accordance with the wishes of the newly formed groups within the framework of their political system. But in many of the developing societies the new formations have been perceived as a threat to the unity and integrity of the Nation-State system. Academics have started analysing various aspects of the activities of the ethnic groups and the activities of the state system to maintain unity[7]. The interactive process of the Nation-State with ethnic groups has brought about several changes in the polity of the nation, the regions and the ethnic groups[8]. Pulling and pushing forces towards the Nation-State and the ethnic groups will always go on in the name of ethnic identity and national identity.

It was believed that the formation of ethnic identity would be always detrimental to the formation of national identity and *vice versa*[9]. Later it was proved that dual identities in a Nation-State need not necessarily works against each other. Both identities can be maintained for the advantage of both without affecting the interests of the nation and the ethnic groups. The complementarily of both the identities is not properly perceived in India[10]. Hence the assimilation of ethnic people in the mainstream is slow.

The concept of nation has been re-defined while, on the other hand, for the formation of ethnic identity among the people, a variety of symbols like language, culture, religion or tribe have been used. Since the modern Nation-State system has given the people the idea that it has got power and resources for distribution, in order to maximise the benefits and to get due share in the national resources, groups have been formed. Leaders who were at the helm of affairs used to highlight the pride of the nation and state while ethnic advocates used to highlight the plight of the ethnic groups. The activities of the collectivities have increased in scale and the anchorage of the identity has become very strong in many groups. Ethnic symbols enabled the academics to justify the usage of the concept of nation by the ethnic groups[11]. Yet distinctions were maintained between ethnic groups and the Nation-State. At present conflicts and wars are not so much among the Nation-State as among the collectivities. Development and its consequences have propelled groups to intensify the ethnic polarisation by their activities to get their due share in national allocation of resources and in power.

In India national identity formation has become one of the interesting subjects of historians, sociologists and anthropologists. Looking at the process of identity historically, there are three patterns of identity formation or linking people with national identity[12]. They are referred to as hegemonic, uniformity-pattern and pluralist. From the Aryan migration to the freedom struggle, activities were continuously geared up for identity formation based on religion, culture, language, common land and so on. It is a process by which people are oriented to look at issues from a standpoint. The exercise or orientation would be done by a variety of forces in a democratic society. People would be in the midst of pulling forces and pushing forces. In India even before the formation of the Nation-State, forces were on to lay a foundation to divide the country into ethnic nations for which the colonial masters were helpful[13]. After independence steps have been taken to cement the segmented forces. Yet, problems persist in many parts of the country. Tamil Nadu was one among the provinces where ethnic culture was perpetuated.

This study analyse how the Indian state is being viewed by the Tamils and how people exhibit their loyalty towards the nation despite the presence of many ethnic groups. Well defined attributes have been fixed for analysing ethnic identity and loyalty and national identity and loyalty. Totally fifteen attributes are identified as indicators of loyalty towards the Nation-State[14]. They are: extending moral support to the federal government during the crisis of the nation, contributing money or material resources during periods of economic crisis either due to war or natural calamity, taking pride in declaring ourself an Indian citizen, respecting the symbols of the country, participating in national celebrations, respecting the

Constitution, and cherishing the contributions of the founding fathers of the country to building the nation. The detail of the reactions of the respondents to these attributes are given hereunder.

People should have a strong feeling that they belong to a particular nation. They should feel proud of calling themselves citizens of this country. Against this background a question was asked as to whether they are proud of calling themselves citizens of this country. To this, as per, Table 6.1, 70 per cent responded positively stating that they are proud of calling themselves Indian citizens. Here it is to be noted that while giving such positive reply to this question, they have attributed reasons for such pride. They have given four or five concrete reasons. Indians have got an exemplary tolerant attitude; they lead a life for other; they perpetuate democracy; though they are illiterate and ignorant they maintain unity despite the differences in terms of culture, language, religion, caste, colour, region and food habits; and, the art of living was evolved only on Indian soil and this is the main contribution of Indian society to the world. But 29 per cent said that they don't have such a pride. It does not, however, mean that they are against the nation.

Table 6.1 : Respondents Proud of Being Indians

Sl. No.	Category	No. of Respondents	Percentage
1.	Yes	281	70.25
2.	No	119	29.75
	Total	400	100.00

Source : Computed.

Normal during the period of ethnic identity formation a variety of strategies are used by the ethnic makers to influence the attitude and belief of the people towards the ethnic group[15]. In the Indian context they have projected the Indian state as the real stumbling block for the progress of the ethnic groups. Indian state has been characterized as the symbol of domination perpetuating hegemonic activities. The domination of the minority over the majority has pushed the groups from the mainstream and consolidated their position in the respective regions. In the process people have started losing faith in the Nation-State and gaining faith in ethnic group activities. Against this background one has to look at the loyalty of the people towards the nation. In order to test the loyalty of the people towards the nation the respondents were asked to what extent they would extend their support to the federal government when the whole country is facing a crisis.

Table 6.2 : Supporting the Federal Government during Time of Crisis

Sl. No.	Category	No. of Respondents	Percentage
1.	Full Support	323	80.70
2.	No Support	77	19.30
	Total	400	100.00

Source : Computed.

To this question 80 per cent of the respondents according to Table 6.2, replied that they will extend full cooperation to the federal government when it is facing a crisis. Many of them quoted the DMK's approach adopted at the time of the Chinese aggression. The DMK then adopted a resolution to give up the demand for a separate Tamil Nadu for Tamils. Further they quoted that, after the assassination of Rajiv Gandhi, Tamils in Tamil Nadu stopped assisting the extremists in Sri Lanka.

There is yet another indicator of supporting the federal government not only morally but also materially when it faces a crisis due to aggression or a threat from another country or due to natural calamity, when people used to contribute liberally to the war fund or natural calamity fund. The respondents were asked to what extent they are committed to the nation by contributing money to crisis funds. To this 78.2 per cent of the respondents according to Table 6.3, said that they have contributed money at times of war or natural calamity, while 21.8 per cent said that they have not contributed anything to the federal government during times of crisis. It is interesting to note that many of the other regions and provinces have not taken so much of effort as Tamil Nadu to collect war fund or natural calamity fund. This region has given more than what other regions have contributed to the war fund or natural calamity fund. This was repeatedly cited by the respondents in their interaction with the field staff.

Table 6.3 : Whether Respondents' Conbribute to War or Calamity Fund

Sl. No.	Category	No. of Respondents	Percentage
1.	Yes	271	67.75
2.	No	129	32.25
	Total	400	100.00

Source : Computed.

Respecting the Constitution is another indicator of loyalty towards the nation. In this study 80 per cent of the respondents said that they respect the Constitution of India, while 20 per cent said that they do not respect it. When the Constitution is not respected by the leaders of the country at the centre and the state, one cannot expect from ordinary citizens that they should respect the Constitution. This question has got special significance as the ethnic political organisation had disrespected the Constitution by burning copies of it and the leaders had felt that this kind of activities alone would arouse popular sentiments against the nation. On all the occasions the leaders were taken into police custody. Cases were registered against them. Hence attention was drawn towards this issue.

Yet, another question was posed to the respondents to evaluate their national loyalty. During the time of conflict between the State and the Centre on an issue affecting the life of the people, 78 per cent of the respondents as per Table 6.4, said that they would support the state government and they would not extend their support to the Nation-State. Only 21 per cent of the respondents replied that national interest is foremost and hence they would extend their support to the federal government. The respondents quoted certain events and incidents to justify their stand. When the state government was not able to get the due share of rice from the central pool the chief minister observed a fast and during such occasions it is necessary that the state interest has to be protected and hence they said that they supported the chief minister. Their priority would be the state.

Table 6.4 : Respondents Response during Conflict between Centre and State

Sl. No.	Category	No. of Respondents	Percentage
1.	Centre	86	21.50
2.	State	314	78.50
	Total	400	100.00

Source : Computed.

There is yet another indicator, namely, respecting the symbols of the Nation-State. Respecting the national anthem and the national flag was taken as an indicator. The respondents have responded to this question in Table 6.5. 72.5 per cent of the respondents said that consciously they respect the national flag and the national anthem. The respondents stated that they had been oriented initially by the freedom fighters after independence and later they were equally oriented to respect the Tamil anthem called "Tamil Thai Vazhthu". It is a song sung in all government functions like the National Anthem. They respect both the national anthem and the Tamil Thai Vazhthu. However, 27.5 per cent of the respondents replied that they did not disrespect the national flag or the national anthem but added that they are not conscious of the importance of the national flag and the national anthem.

Table 6.5 : Respecting National Flag and National Anthem

Sl. No.	Category	No. of Respondents	Percentage
1.	Yes	290	72.5
2.	No	110	27.5
	Total	400	100.00

Source : Computed.

Recongnising the contributions made by the founding father to building the nation is yet another indicator of national loyalty. The respondents were questioned on this.

Table 6.6 : Recognising and Respecting Conbribution of Founding Fathers

Sl. No.	Category	No. of Respondents	Percentage
1.	Yes	330	82.5
2.	No	70	17.5
	Total	400	100.00

Source : Computed.

According to Table 6.6, 82.5 per cent of the respondents replied that they do recognise the contributions made by the founding fathers to building the nation and the sacrifice made by the freedom fighters to liberate the country. Only 17.5 per cent of respondents have no special liking for freedom fighters. The respondents were unequivocal in recognising the contributions and sacrifices made by the freedom fighters and founding fathers of the country in liberating the society from the colonial yoke and carving out a nation for Indians. While recognising the services of those leaders the respondents argued that freedom from the British was not obtained for the domination of the minority over the majority by adopting a social hierarchy. To liberate the oppressed from internal colonialism they moved over to various ethnic groups. The respondents have indicated the demands of the ethnic groups which are related to the social and economic problems of the people. Among various legitimate approaches to problems aligning with an ethnic group is also one. Mere articulation of demands to the Nation-State under the direction of the ethnic group does not connote any feeling against the Nation-State.

Organising, participating in and attending important national celebrations such as Independence Day, Republic Day, birth and death anniversary of Mahatma Gandhi are considered indicators of identifying with the nation. Questions were asked in this regard.

Table 6.7 : Organising, Participating and Attending National Celebrations

Sl. No.	Category	No. of Respondents	Percentage
1.	Yes	220	55.0
2.	No	180	45.0
	Total	400	100.00

Source : Computed.

As per Table 6.7, 55 per cent of the respondents unequivocally replied that they used to participate in such functions organised by institutions, while 45 per cent of the respondents said that they have no special interest in it. They used to attend the regular activities but they are not being invited by their organisers. Some of the respondents said that such celebrations were very attractive during the 50s and 60s and after that there has been no such attractive show. Schools and public institution were instructed to celebrate these occasions even in remote villages during those days. But, now, these institutions declare holidays. In this scenario the public cannot be expected to organise such celebrations and participate in these programmes. But ethnic political parties have organised several such functions in order to remember the sacrifice made by the leaders to develop ethnic organisation and to celebrate the birth and death anniversaries of the ethnic leaders. These programmes and activities are so attractive that they draw the attention of all. Opportunities are more for the respondents to attend these meetings and programmes of ethnic organisations. There is no such spirit among the national institutions and leaders. In order to keep up the vibrancy among the people in perpetuating ethnic activities ethnic organisations constantly keep in touch with the people.

To identify the anchorage of identity several questions were asked and the responses are given hereunder.

Table 6.8 : Preferred Identity for Reference

Sl. No.	Category	No. of Respondents	Percentage
1.	National	91	22.75
2.	Regional	63	15.75
3.	Ethnic	101	25.25
4.	Caste	116	29.00
5.	Religious	29	7.25
	Total	400	100.00

Source : Computed.

As per Table 6.8, 29 per cent of the respondents stated that they prefer only caste identity and 25 per cent said that they prefer ethnic (Tamil) identity, while 22 per cent said that they prefer only national identity. When asked for the reasons for preferring such identity all the respondents said that the preferred identity helps them to get economic, social and political gains in the existing socio-political environment in the state.

While analysing the national loyalty question based on the responses of the respondents, it is observed that seventy to eighty per cent of the respondents have commitment and loyalty towards the nation. To exhibit their loyalty they have committed themselves to various kinds of activities. Their integrity and loyalty cannot be questioned as they have shown through their activities. At the same time they maintain the ethnic identity for their socio-economic and political gains.

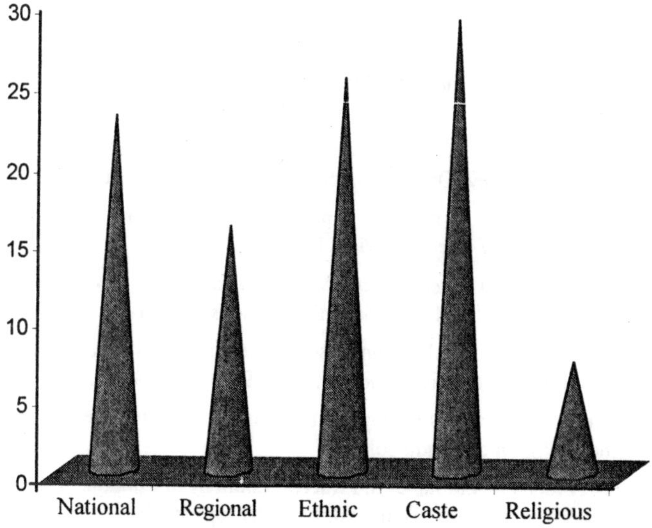

Fig. 6.1 : Preferred Identity for Reference

NOTES AND REFERENCES

1. Crawford Young, *The Political of Cultural Pluralism,* Madison : The University of Wisconsin Press, 1976, p. 14.

2. From Hayes to Smith, An array of books and articles have been published in the same area. For more details see Careton Hayes, *The Historical Evolution of Modern Nationalism,* New York: Richard R. Smith, 1931, A.D. Smith National Identity, Harmondsworth: Penguin, 1991.

3. For a detailed analysis see Paul Brass, *Religion, Language and Politics in North India,* Cambridge: Cambridge University Press, 1974.

4. John Hutchinson and Anthony, D. Smith, *Ethnicity,* New York: Oxford University Press, 1996.

5. Paul R. Brass, "Ethnic Groups and Ethnic Identity Formation," in *Ethnicity* (eds.) John Hutchinson and Anthony D. Smith, New York: Oxford University Press, 1996.

6. A.D. Smith, *Nations and Nationalism in a Global Era,* Cambridge: Polity Press, 1995.

7. Steven Tagil (ed.), *Societies and New States;* New York: Free Press, 1963.

8. Clifford M. Geetz (ed.), *Societies and New States;* New York: Free Press, 1963.

9. Walker Connor, "Nation Building or Nation Destroying", *World Politics,* 24:3 (1972).

10. G. Palanithurai and R. Thandavan (ed.). *Perspective on Indian Regionalism,* New Delhi: Kanishka Publishers and Distributors, 1993.

11. Walker Connor, "A nation is a nation, is a state is an ethnic group, is a..." *Ethnic and Racial Studies*, 1:4 (1978).

12. T. K. Oommen, *Citizenship and National Identity : From Colonialism to Globalization,* New Delhi: Sage Publications, pp. 14-36.

13. C.H. Enloe "Internal Colonialism, Federalism and Alternative State Development Strategies," *Publics*, 7:4 (1977).

14. In this study focus is on loyalty towards the Nation-State not towards Hindu religion or Hindu culture.

15. A.B. Anderson, and James S. Frideres, *Ethnicity in Canada : Theoretical Perspective,* Toronto : Butterworths, 1981, pp. 36-51.

16. P. Worseley, *The Three Worlds : Culture and Word Developments*, Chicago: Chicago University Press, 1984.

7

INTEGRATED ANALYSIS

Ethnicity is a sense of ethnic identity. An ethnic group is one that uses symbols like culture and language to bring about cohesion among the people and to form a self-conscious community to include and exclude members with the objective of establishing the well-being of the members of the group[1]. Ethnic group identity involves a claim to status and recognition either as a superior group or as a group at least equal to other groups. Ethnicity is an alternative form of social organisation and identification of class but it is a contingent and changeable status. Ethnic groups that use ethnicity to make demands in the political arena for allocation in their status, in their educational opportunities are engaged in a form of interest group politics which seeks to improve the well-being of group members as individuals. An ethnic group aspires to national status and recognition. It has many phases. It will move up to satisfy the, economic and social demands, failing which it will move to pose a demand for establishing control over a territory within the nation and finally, it will move towards the declaration of a demand for a sovereign independent state for its members. A nation, therefore, may be seen as a particular type of ethnic community or rather as an ethnic community political with recognised group rights in the political system[2].

Nations may be created by the transformation of an ethnic group in a multi-ethnic state into a self-conscious political entity or by the amalgamation of diverse groups and the formation of an interethnic composite or homogeneous national culture through the agency of the modern state. The two processes of transformation seem to be the same but there are different starting points[3]. Arguments, explanations and interpretations of the two processes are different and they gain recognition when the majority of the groups and collectivities endorse the explanations and interpretations. Péople are always in the hands of the leaders and the organisations.

In the historical process how people are concientised towards a particular set of symbols determines the identity of the people. It need not necessarily mean that all people will move towards a particular set of symbols and institutions. One can find a trend in the formation of identity as the majority could move towards certain symbols which may help the people to have a Nation-State identity or an ethnic identity. The two identities are different. Sometimes the identity of people towards Nation-State will be dominant and stronger than the identity of people towards ethnicity and *vice versa*. Apart from the two distinct identities, people may have dual identities and multiple identities. Identities are being used for the socio-economic advantage of the individuals and groups[4]. Identity of an individual and group can be seen in a context. Identity has got intensity. In a particular context one identity may be visible in the activities of the individual and the others remain in sub time form. The sub time identity may become visible in another context. Exhibition of identity depends on the happening of events in a context. Identity has its own anchorage and longevity.

It is natural that the activities of either institutions or the state should inculcate the values of their own with the intention of keeping the people under their fold. The Nation-State is always interested in maintaining the unity and integrity of the nation. It would continuously inject the spirit of patriotism in the minds of the people. It does the function of equalization of communities. It involves itself in the process of cementing the segmented forces[5]. Leaders of groups concientise the individuals about their conditions and positions. In order to keep their identity, the leaders use certain symbols like language, culture and heritage common to them[6]. They are concientised to keep their group identity and to pose demands to the state. The state, through its machinery, takes the initiative to respond to the demands of the groups and to inculcate the values Nation-State and try to keep them within the framework of the Nation-State. The two processes of forming identity and mobilising the Nation-State take place simultaneously along with the process of concientising the people on forming the Nation-State for better living. The members of the group may get themselves strongly identified with the ethnic organisation to maximise their socio-economic benefits or the members of the group may get convinced by the arguments projected by the Nation-State and join the government in solving the problems of the people. The leaders' role in the process of conflict as well as assimilation is inevitable and important.

In the multi-polar world, there are different kinds of strategies adopted by ethnic groups to form identity among the members, to project their ethnic demands and to bargain with the Nation-State and equally the Nation-State will adopt a variety of strategies to manage the ethnic conflict and make the ethnic groups assimilate in the mainstream[7]. There are groups totally assimilate in the mainstream in the world and there are groups still fighting for secession. A number of groups have got independence also.

Generally in the process of identity formation and activity initiation either in the domain of ethnicity or in the domain of nation-building (building the Nation-State) there will be always a tough competition among the leaders or elites. They compete with each other in mobilising the people towards their objective of forming identity. The course and intensity of the activities of the group or people depends on the strategies and sagacity of the leaders of the ethnic group and the Nation-State.

Further the ethnic group activities need not necessarily be under one leadership. It can have many organisations and institutions. To represent a particular group there may be different organisations working together or fighting against each other. The activities of ethnic groups may also be influenced by the contextual factors. In the course of years due to weak leadership or owing to some other reasons, some of the organisations may become out of date. Some of the leaders of the ethnic groups and the Nation-State may become unpopular. New organisations and new leaders may emerge contextually and they may have a firm grip over the issues. For political activities people are mobilised by different ethnic organisations but people have perspectives perceptions, views, attitudes on issues and events. The fast changing socio-economic scenario alters the perceptions of the people and thereby their identity will also be changed. The ethnic groups at present are not raising the issues in one voice. There are polarisation and conversion of the groups into political organisations. The political organisations subsequently develop cracks and divide into many, focusing on the same issues for their polity. In this context the views, perceptions and attitudes of the people on those issues matter much more than the opinions of the parties and leaders.

India is a land of paradoxes and riddles. It is a plural society having a number of cultural and lingual groups apart from religious groups. The leaders have adopted a variety of strategies to concientise the people about their culture moorings and lingual purity and glory with the aim of forming strong identity on ethnic grounds. The Indian state has been adopting a multiplicity of strategies to pacify them and to keep them under the fold of the Nation-State[8]. Some of the groups have regulated their activities within the framework of the Indian political system. A few of the groups are still pursuing the course of conflict with the Indian state.

Tamil Nadu is one such province which was considered a trouble-prone state. The Tamil ethnic groups were concientised to form Tamil ethnic-identity which is known for its rich and glorious tradition of language and culture. There was an intellectual movement behind the ethnic movement and that was utilised for the political movement. Primarily it was only a cultural and lingual movement with a strong intellectual background[9]. Those who were instrumental in sowing seeds for the intellectual movement had not thought that it would end in a political movement. Simultaneously the liberation movement gained momentum to liberate the nation from the colonial yoke. People were concientised on the concept of nation and freedom, by which the national identity was formed.

After India won freedom, the development process was closely monitored and it was argued that a particular section was exploiting the situation and grabbing the opportunity for prosperity and social upward mobility. Thus a social movement was organised with the strong support of certain sections of the same Tamil society.

In the fast changing economic and political scenario, the older assumptions underwent changes, sometimes radical changes, and, as a result, conventional theories did not have answers to many of the questions. It is necessary to understand the dynamics of the identity of the people and its linkages with the polity of the nation, more particularly the linkage between the identity of the people towards the groups and the identification of the people with Nation-State. Ethnic identity and national loyalty form an important subject. It is assumed that these two kinds of identities of the people will work contradictorily in opposite directions, ultimately resulting in questioning the base of the Nation-State. This kind of assumption has been tested in many societies. At present, identity is perceived in context. Depending on its utility and profitability, identity is being maintained in a particular symbol. It is proved beyond doubt that individuals will maintain multiple identities. Exhibition of identity depends on the contextual benefit accruing to the individuals. But these identities are well within the framework of the Nation-State system.

In this work it is to be investigated to what extent the ethnic identity of the Tamils can be reconciled with the national identity or national loyalty of the same individual. Respondents have given their perception of their loyalty towards the ethnic groups and the Nation-State. To evaluate the ethnic identity, a battery of indicators have been fixed based on theoretical assumptions[10]. Equally to test the national loyalty, a loyalty matrix has been developed. Ethnic loyalty includes their attachment to their mother-tongue, their attitude towards the language, their positioning of the language in the cultural order, following the cultural calendar of activities, celebrating the cultural festivals, educating their wards in the regional medium, looking at the language, primacy of language in economic and social development, considering the ethnic movement as scientific and progressive, perpetuating the view of the neglect of Tamil Nadu by the north and faith in ethnic organisations and parties. Further they maintain the notion that the ethnic political parties are not working against the Indian Nation-State.

In the same way national identity or loyalty has to be assessed through certain indicators. This includes, attachment to the Nation-State, extending support to the federal government during times of crisis, contributing monetarily to the nation when it faces economic crisis or war, respecting the national anthem and the national flag, recognising the contributions made by the founding fathers to the building of modern India and participating in national celebrations.

The details of the responses to these questions are listed hereunder in a capsule.

Sl. No.	Indicators of Identity	Percentage of Respondents
Ethnic Identity		
1.	Attachment to the mother-tongue	92
2.	Equating mother-tongue with mother	88
3.	Worshipping the language	70
4.	Following the Tamil calendar	32
5.	Celebrating Pongal as part of Tamil culture	63
6.	Celebrating cultural festivals with gaiety	60
7.	Sending children to Tamil medium schools	60
8.	Sentiments against Hindi	76
9.	Declaring Tamil a classical language	83
10.	Medium of instruction in schools should be Tamil	78
11.	All transactions in Government and education should be in Tamil	71
12.	Development could be achieved through Tamil	90
13.	Tamil nationalism is always in scientific mode	90
14.	Tamil Nadu is being neglected by the Centre	77
15.	Faith in ethnic political parties	74
16.	Ethnic parties are not against India	68
17.	Supporting the state during the conflict between the Centre and the State	78
National Loyalty		
1.	Proud to call themselves Indians	70

(Contd.)

Sl. No.	Indicators of Identity	Percentage of Respondents
2.	Extending full support to the Central Government during crisis	80
3.	Contributing material to the Central Government during economic crisis	78
4.	Respecting the National Flag	72
5.	Respecting the National Anthem	72
6.	Recognising the contributions of the founding fathers and freedom fighters	82
7.	Participating in National Celebrations	55
Preferred Identity		
1.	Preferring caste identity	29
2.	Preferring ethnic identity	25
3.	Preferring national identity	22
4.	Preferring regional identity	15

It is indisputable that the identity of an individual is shaped by a number of factors. Identity may be of different natures. They are: cultural identity, lingual identity, regional identity, ethnic identity, national identity, religious identity and so on. These identities are formed with varying institutions. Different segments are involved in identity formation. Formed identities are being used by different institutions. Individuals have different kinds of identities and they are being used in context.

In Tamil Nadu attempts were made to socialise the people on the cultural and lingual issues purely for social considerations. When a sizeable section of the population is concientised on those issues, the identity is used for reformation of the society. At a later stage the transformation of the social identity changed to political identity. The British colonial administration, by its policies and approaches, propelled the elites of the communities other than the Brahmins in search of a common identity.

In the process of identification they acquired a common identity for all the communities as "Non-Brahmin". Non-Brahmin is not a group or a community by itself. Since Brahmins were their reference and point of attack, they invented a name, "Non-

Brahmin". Later it was realised that it is not a community by itself and that it cannot last long. Moreover, for Non-Brahmins, a common culture and language could not be found. In this context the western missionaries helped these elites by their contribution in reviving the old glorious of the Tamil language and culture. Missionaries of the west and native sages laid the intellectual foundation for the ethnic movement in Tamil Nadu.

The benefits enjoyed by the Brahmins during the colonial administration and their placement in the social hierarchy propelled the elites of the non-Brahmin communities to take the initiative to form an organisation or association to project their socio-economic demands. This loose association and organisation had different dimensions. Initially it had only cultural and social dimensions and later it developed a political dimension also. Not all the people of these communities were inclined to move towards the ethnic movement. While going through the political history of the province since 1900 one can find a strong supportive group from the same communities inclined towards building the nation or the Nation-State. Among the non-Brahmins one group under the banner of Non-Brahmin Movement, which subsequently became the Dravidian Movement, mobilised the support of the people and made itself a factor or a force to reckon with. The Non-Brahmin Movement adopted a variety of strategies to convince the members of Non-Brahmin communities that the existing political and social arrangement was exploiting the non-Brahmins for the advantage of the Brahmins. But the Non-Brahmin Movement underwent changes and thereby its ideology also changed. Even within the movement there were different formations working against each other although maintaining the same ideological contours. Gradually the movement moved into the framework of party politics. As a result the ethnic movement produced political parties within the movement and these political parties with an ethnic base competed with each other in the provincial politics. For the past thirty years the state politics has been in the hands of the ethnic political parties. Even the national political parties have taken up the issues of the ethnic political parties because the people have been oriented to look at issues from the prospective of the region. Yet they maintain their loyalty towards the nation.

One can see from the responses of the respondents that there is a strong inclination towards ethnic ideology, culture, language and caste. At the same time they have a strong loyalty towards the Nation-State. Their identity towards ethnicity starts with 60 per cent and reaches 92 per cent. Their Nation-State identity starts with 55 per cent and reaches 82 per cent. Keeping a particular identity is always for getting some benefits or even to gain social recognition. They may be against another group but they are not against the state. They strongly believe that it is the responsibility of the Nation-State to equalise the communities. Hence ethnic identity and national identity are not two entities fighting against each other. They are the two sides of the same coin. When this factor is analysed contextually one has to take note of the changes that have crept into the organisations, groups and leaders of the ethnic groups and the Nation-State. Over a period of time demands have changed, priorities have changed, strategies have changed for both the ethnic political parties and the Nation-State. The ethnic movement started with the objective of uplifting the non-Brahmins by breaking the social hierarchical system established by the Brahmins through Hinduism. Initially it opposed only Brahmins and got the support of the colonial masters. After independence it opposed the Indian National Congress and the Nation-State as the federal government and provincial government were under the sway of the Indian National Congress. Till 1967, ethnic group activities were very intensive and aggressive. After 1967, their demands and the intensity of their activities were not so aggressive as they were before. After 1967, there was a schism in the ethnic political party and they fought against each other and aligned with national political forces and threreby the very character of the ethnic political party has changed. Ethnic group members were oriented to look at the Brahmin community and the federal government and government institutions as enemies of non-Brahmins as they were all citadels of the Brahmins. But, after 1967, such perception has changed as the ethnic political parties aligned with national political parties with the sole aim of keeping themselves in power. The ethnic organisations and parties have given up Dravidianism, Tamil nationalism, anti-Brahminism, opposing the imposition of Hindi, and the demand for State autonomy. But people still have faith in all these issues. Those who oriented the masses on these issues have changed their attitude and perception. In order to retain the power base the ethnic political parties have started adopting populist policies on a competitive basis. One can trace the transformation of the ethnic group into an ethnic movement and from ethnic movement into ethnic political party. Subsequently the ethnic political party splits and there are a number of ethnic political parties. As long as an ethnic group maintains its solidarity and ideology, the group, however small, has its own strength and power to bargain with the government. When it becomes a movement, its bargaining strength increases. If the movement transforms itself into a political party, its base is expanded and it will become a part of the political system, especially in the decision-making process. But necessarily it has to channelise its activities well within the framework of the political system. In the process of ethnic conflict management, the ethnic political party has to face the challenges of the state system. Keeping the party intact is always in the hands of the leaders of the ethnic political party. Aspirations towards power and position propel the leaders to split the party and form separate political parties. Such kinds of activities weaken the ideological position of the ethnic political parties. In order to keep the position in politics, the parties cannot take a tough stand against the federal government but they adopt retrograde policies towards the ethnic groups.

To safeguard the interests of the party, the ethnic political party has to align with the national parties which had been totally opposing the ideological plank of the ethnic political party. In the process the ethnic political parties are disempowered and they cannot orient the people in the ideological contours of ethnicity. The so-called major issues like language and culture are relegated to the background. Members of the ethnic group realise the weak position of the parties and they adopt a moderate course of action. The leaders of ethnic political parties, for their own advantage, talk about lacklustre ethnic issues which do not attract the people. Slowly people form the notion that the politics of ethnicity is to maximise benefits and hence they too develop multiple identity. While looking at the responses of the respondents in this study on their identity, one can see the perfect blend of ethnic identity with national loyalty.

They have strong commitment towards ethnicity and they are equally committed to the nation. Thus the higher the commitment to ethnicity the higher the commitment to the nation. In the formative years, when people were oriented in ethnicity, people were very strong in their commitment to the ethnic group, negating the principles of the Nation-State.

The colonial administration never involved itself in the process of ethnic equalization by its policies. In the formative years after independence, looking at issues from the perspective of ethnicity was considered improper and unscientific. The Nation-State authorities felt that it would weaken the nation-building process. They relised the implications of such an approach only at a later stage. Hence, the politics pursued by the federal government were instrumental for the ethnic group to concientise the group members on ethnic lines. But the ethnic consciousness got diffused only at a large stage as the ethnic political organisation could not move further in the ethnic plank. In the thick of ethnic political activities three decades have gone. Over the years a spectacular transformation has taken place in Tamil society. By projecting the Tamil and Dravidian identity, the ethnic political organisation bargained with the federal government. By adopting the same methodology the Tamil identity was broken into caste identity and caste groups consolidated their position and started bargaining with the state government which is managed by either one of the ethnic political parties (DMK or AIADMK).

Thus the colonial policies and the policies of the government in independent India paved the way for the formation of ethnic group identity to articulate their grievances for redressal. The intellectual background prepared by various individuals and organisations in the social and cultural domain were used by the ethnic group leaders to sensitise the masses on ethnic issues. By mobilising the masses the ethnic organisations gained strength to bagain with the federal government and the state government. To manage the problems of the ethnic groups the state authorities adopted a variety of approaches and thereby they were drawn towards governance and closer to the political system and administration. When the ethnic group moved over to politics by changing its character, approach and ideology, the activities of the ethnic political party were brought under the framework of the political system. As a result intense competition for power developed which ultimately paved the way for split and proliferation of parties with the same plank. In the process, the people perceived that ethnic polity is only an instrument to gain something. So they adopted multiple identity to bargain with the centre and the state. They now have local caste identity, ethnic identity and national, identity. All this is only a political expression.

NOTES AND REFERENCES

1. John Vincent, "The Structuring of Ethnicity," *Human Organisation,* XXIII:4 (Winter 1974), pp. 376-377.
2. Karl W. Deutsch and William, J. Foltz (eds.), *Nation Building,* New York: Atherton, Press, 1966.
3. Paul R. Brass, *Ethnicity and Nationalism: Theory and Comparison,* New Delhi: Sage Publications; 1991, pp. 20-21.
4. Paul R. Brass, "Ethnic Groups and Ethnic Identity Formation," in *Ethnicity* (eds.) John Hutchinson, and Anthony D. Smith, New York : Oxford University, Press, 1966, p. 87.
5. I. Lustick, "Deeply Divided Societies: Consociationalism *versus* Control," *World Politics,*31:3 (April 1979) pp. 325-344 and C.H. Enloe, "Central Government's Strategies for Coping with Separatist Movements," In W.H. Morris Jones (ed.). *The Politics of Separatism,* London: University of London Institute of Commonwealth Studies Collected Seminars Papers, No. 19, 1976.
6. H. Gans, "Symbolic Ethnicity: The Future of Ethnic Groups and Cultures in America," *Ethnic and Racial Studies,* 2(1979), pp. 1-20.
7. David Brown, "Ethnicity, Nationalism and Democracy in South East Asia," *Ethnicity* (eds.) John Hutchinson and Anthony D. Smith, New York: Oxford University Press, 1996, pp. 306-307.
8. Paul R. Brass, *Ethnicity and Nationalism : Theory and Comparison,* New Delhi: Sage Publications, 1991, pp. 142-146.
9. Eugene F. Irschick, *Tamil Revivalism in the 1930s,* Chennai : Cre-A, 1986.
10. These assumptions are based on the arguments of Anthony D. Smith, For more details see Anthony D. Smith, *The Ethnic Origin of Nations,* Oxford: Basil Blackwell, 1986.

8

CONCLUSION

It is evident from the reports that have been produced all over the world on ethnicity that wars between Nation-States have decreased and conflicts between and among communities have increased claimed the lives of millions of people in the world. The developed technology, especially in the domain of communication, has helped to make profit but, at the same time, the developed technology communication have increased conflicts in the world. It was presumed in the beginning that the communication development would eradicate differences and pave the way for nation building. But the communication developed worked contradictorily in society. The ethnic phenomenon crept into both developed a developing societies. Studies were undertaken by both governmental and non-governmental organisations in different areas of ethnicity, namely ethnic group formation, ethnic identity, ethnic conflict, ethnic conflict management, ethnopolitics, ethnocentrism, ethno-nationalism, ethnography and so on. A variety of approaches; models, simulations frameworks and theories have been developed. In the formative years of ethnic research, everyone believed that the ethnic phenomenon anti-Nation-State as nation building was the primary objective and activity of the new societies which had been liberated from shackles of colonial yoke. But the trend changed when more number of ethnic groups remained in the framework of the Nation-States and assimilated in the mainstream. Approaches have further changed after witnessing the development achieved by different ethnic groups by acting on the ethnic plank. It was realised that ethnicity need not be construed as working against the Nation-State. Instead it came to be seen as a strategy or an instrument to achieve development. Initially the concept of patriotism, nationalism and national loyalty gained currency among the scholars and they conducted research without juxtaposing the concept of ethnic identity. Ethnic identity was considered as negative to nation-building. But arguments have been developed that individuals have multiple identities, that the identities have varied intensity, and that, depending on the need, people use their various identities.

In the present study the old proposition has been taken for examination. Basically the Dravidian Movement was conceived in different dimensions and it was studied by scholars, both native and western, with different approaches. All the old propositions were tested. Some of the propositions were invalidated and a few were validated. Of the validated propositions the continuing ethnic fervour among the people in Tamil Nadu has given some validity to the proposition that Tamil ethnic identity need not necessarily be a negative factor, that it can go well with national identity and that national loyalty need not be diminished. Hence, this study has analysed the interface between ethnic identity and national loyalty. In Tamil society ethnic identity was formed through the concerted effort of the intellectuals and ethnic leaders over the years, for which the colonial administration as well as the early Indian administration were responsible. The colonial administration sowed the seeds. The early Government of India was equally responsible for not initiating steps to mitigate the ethnic fervour.

The conversion of the ethnic movement into a political party provided opportunity for the govermnent at the centre to bring the ethnic political party within the framework of the political system. In the conversion process political ambitions were developed among the leaders which ultimately resulted in proliferation of political parties on the same ethnic plank: On a competitive basis the ethnic political parties have mobilised the masses on ethnic issue but they compete with each other with the support of nationalist forces which ultimately results in the congruence of ethnic identity and national identity and loyalty. The results of the study show that the respondents are having high ethnic identity as well as loyalty towards the nation. The identified traits of ethnic identity and national loyalty are present in the same individuals. They retain their ethnic identity to maximise their profit. Their attachment to ethnic values and national values are equally high. During the crises of the nation they are with the nation. During conflicts between the State and Centre they go with the state. Still the respondents believe that they can develop only by being attached to the ethnic values the Tamil community. At the same time they believe that development can be achieved well within the framework of the Indian nation. They still hold the feeling that the federal government is not well disposed towards the Tamil province for its development. They value the contributions made by the national leaders for the cause of the nation. Equally they value the contributions made by the ethnic political parties which competing with each other to seek power, so that they can bargain with the Centre. This is the considered opinion of the respondents.

ANNEXURE-I

ETHNIC IDENTITY AND NATIONAL LOYALTY : A CASE STUDY OF TAMIL NADU

I. Socio-Economic Background

1. Name :

2. Age :

20-30	31-40	40-50	51 & ABOVE

3. Sex :

MALE	FEMALE

4. Education :

ILL	PRI	SEC	COLL	OTHERS

5. Profession :

AGRI	BUSI	INDUS	TEACH	OTHERS

6. Income per annum (Thousands) :

0-20	21-40	41-60	61 & ABOVE

7. Wealth :

0-100000	100001-200000	200001 & ABOVE

8. Community :

SC	ST	MBC	BC	FC

9. Religion :

HINDU	MUSLIM	CHRIST

10. Settlement :

URBAN	RURAL

11. Membership in Organisation :

CASTE	TRADE	TEACHERS	FANS CLUB

II. Political Socialization

12. When did you aware of politics? (in age)

5-10	11-15	16-20	21-30	31 & ABOBE

13. Through whom you came to know about politics?

PARENTS	FRIENDS	PRESS	POLITICAL ORGANISATIONS

SCHOOL MATES

14. Is any of your family member involved in politics?

YES	NO

15. What kind of newspaper do you read?

GENERAL PAPER	PARTY PAPER	ALL PAPERS

16. Do you have close friends who have strong political affiliation?

YES	NO

17. Has anybody from your community actively involved in politics?

YES	NO

18. Did you get any political experience during your school days?

YES	NO

19. How often you use to discuss political issues in the friends circle and with your family members

FREQUENTLY	OCCASIONALLY	NEVER

20. Do you have the practice of influencing your family members during the election for the benefit of a political organisation?

YES	NO

21. Do you maintain permanent political identity for several years?

YES	NO

III. Political Participation

22. Are you a member in a political party?

YES	NO

23. If yes, is it a National/Regional Party? (Mention the party)

24. When did you become a member of this party? (Mention the year)

25. Why did you choose this party?

IDEOLOGY	LEADER ATTRACTION

FAMILY LOYALTY	COMPULSION

26. Who motivated you to join politics ?

PARENTS	FRIENDS	PARTY LEADERS	ON HIS OWN

27. What is your position in this party?

MERE MEMBERSHIP	ACTIVIST	LEADER	OTHER

28. Will you take part in the activities of your party?

YES	NO

29. If yes, in what kind of activities, you are involved?

30. Are your family members belong to any political party?

YES	NO

31. Specify your level of involvement in political process.

Sl.No.	Name of the Occasion	Never	Occasionally	Frequently
1.	General Elections			
2.	Party Elections			
3.	Conferences			
4.	Party Protest Activities			
5.	Leaders Birthday Celebration			

32. Have you ever gone to jail in support of your party activities?

YES	NO

33. If yes, on what occasion?

34. Did you participate in the previous general elections?

YES	NO

35. Are you a regular reader of the message given by your party leader?

YES	NO

36. Do you contribute money for your party periodically?

YES	NO

37. Have you ever changed over your party loyalty?

YES	NO

38. If yes, why?

39. How many times you have changed over your loyalty?

ONE	TWO	THREE

IV. Ethnic Identity

40. Are you a member in your caste organisation?

YES	NO

41. Do you identify yourself with your caste?

YES	NO

42. Do you have special liking for your language?

YES	NO

43. Do you equate your language with mother ?

YES	NO

44. Are you aware of Tamil Thai Vazhthu?

YES	NO

45. Do you follow the rituals and ceremonies based on Hindu religion in conducting social function in your family?

YES	NO

46. If no, state the reasons?

47. Do you follow the Tamil Calendar for your activities?

48. If no, why?

49. Do you give paramount importance to Pongal celebration?

YES	NO

50. If yes, state the reasons.

51. Will you put your children in English medium schools for their education

YES	NO

52. If no, why?

53. At present which language do you accept at National level?

ENGLISH	HINDI

54. If English, why don't you accept Hindi?

55. Do you agree to make Tamil as a national language?

YES	NO

56. Please specify your opinion about the following statements :

Sl. No.	Items	Agree	Disagree
1.	Land ownership only for Tamilians		
2.	Employment opportunity only for Tamilians		
3.	Tamil people purchase only in Tamilian shops		
4.	Medium of education through Tamil		
5.	Tamil in all aspects		
6.	Tamil identity is affected by CBSE		
7.	All languages should be nationalized		

57. Do you say that Tamil identity is the main reason for DMK capturing power in 1967?

YES	NO

58. Are you aware of the steps taken by the Dravidian government to improve the Tamil language since 1967?

59. Are you aware Dravidian parties played a major role four times (1969, 1979, 1989 and 1996) in forming the government at the centre?

YES	NO

60. If yes, what were the steps taken to develop Tamil language?

61. Who is a Tamilian?

62. Would you like to identify individual by language?

YES	NO

63. Would you like to identify individual by language?

YES	NO

64. Would you like to identify individual by Religion & Culture?

YES	NO

65. What is the difference between Dravidian and Tamilian?

66. Who is an Indian?

67. Do you feel that by using Tamil, development could be achieved in all spheres?

68. Would you allow the Tamils to learn Hindi when employment opportunity are abundant in Hindi Belt?

YES	NO

69. Would you approve of the usage of the concept "Dravida" at present?

YES	NO

70. If yes, why Tamil is being used in every walk of life?

71. Do you mean to say that Tamil language and Tamil culture will develop the Tamil Society in all respects?

72. Do you feel that there is a contradiciton between the Dravidian Movement and Dravidian Parties?

73. Is it not a fact that Tamil Nationalism moves only in tradition negating scientific approach?

74. Is it a fact that the Dravidian Movement used only scientific approach to social issues?

75. What were the effects of Hindi Agitation (1937-1994) organised by Dravidian Parties at different periods?

76. What is wrong if one learns Hindi?

77. What were the steps taken to stop the propaganda of Hindi done by the following organisation/Media/Units

    (a) Hindi Prachara Sabha:

    (b) N.C.C. Training Parade:

    (c) Influence of Hindi films:

    (d) Television programmes:

78. Do you feel that Tami Nadu is neglected by the centre in developmental activities?

YES	NO

79. Do you have full faith in ethnic political parites for the progerss of this province?

YES	NO

80. Would you approve of the anti-natioanl activities of ethnic political party leaders?

YES	NO

81. What will be your action when there is a conflict between the centre and the state?

82. Are you an admirer of your culture?

83. Are you an admirer of your language?

84. Don't you feel the dress and food habits have been thoroughly changed in Tamil Society?

85. Don't you think that the atheiscult has been slowly going down?

86. Why should parties withdraw their principles at the time of emergency?

V. Naitonal Loyalty

87. To whom you will extend your support when the nation is in crisis?

GOVERNMENT	YOUR PARTY

88. Will you stand when the national anthem is sung?

YES	NO

89. Will you sing national anthem?

YES	NO

90. Will you contribute donations to the Central Government to protect the country during emergency?

YES	NO

91. Have you ever contributed war fund during Chinese aggression in 1962 and Pakistan war in 1972?

YES	NO

92. Would you respect the Constitution ?

YES	NO

93. Are you proud of calling yourself an Indian?

YES	NO

94. Which identity you will cherish more for your reference?

NATIONAL	REGIONAL	ETHNIC	CASTE	RELIGIONS

95. Will you accept that by maintaining unity among the Indians poverty could be alleviated and prosperity could be achieved?

YES	NO

96. Are you aware of the services made by Rajaji, VOC, Bharathi?

YES	NO

97. Had they not attracted you?

98. Do you have the practice of participating in the Republic Day Celebration?

YES	NO

99. Do you have the practice of the participating in the Independence Day Celebration?

YES	NO

100. Do you feel that our freedom won by the sacrifice of our leaders?

YES	NO

BIBLIOGRAPHY

Arooran, Nambi, *Tamil Renaissance ane Dravidian Nationalism 1905-1944,* Madurai : Koodal Publishers, 1980.

Annamalai E., *Language Movement in India,* Mysore: Central Institute of Indian Languages, 1979.

Annadurai, C.N., *Thambikku Annavin Kadithangal (Tamil),* Vols. I-XII, Chennai: Paarinilayam, 1981.

Annadurai, C.N., *Tamilarin Marumalarchi (Tamil).* Madras: Paarinilayam, 1975.

Anderson, A.B. and Frideres, J.S., *Ethnicity in Canada: Theoretical Perspectives,* Toronto: Butterworths, 1981.

Barth, Frederick, *Ethnic Groups and Boundaries,* Boston: Little Brown Company, 1980.

Barnett, M.R., *The Politics of Cultural Nationalism in South India,* Princeton: Princeton University Press, 1976.

Beling, Williard and Tolten, George O. (eds.), *Developing Nations: Quest for a Model,* New York: Wiley, 1970.

Beteille, Andre, "Caste in Contemporary India," in *Caste Today* (ed.) C.J. Fuller, New Delhi: Oxford University Press, 1997.

Bhaskaran, S., *Issues in Federalism : Problems of National Integration in Indian and Canadian Federal Systems —A Research Design,* Paper presented at the Indo-Canadian Workshop, Hyderabad, 1981.

Brass, Paul R. (ed.), *Ethnic Groups and the State,* London: Croom Helm, 1985.

Brass, Paul R., "Ethnic Groups and Ethnic Indentity Formation," in *Ethnicity* (ed.) John Hutchinson and Anthony D. Smith, New York: Oxford University Press, 1996.

Brass, Paul R., *Ethnicity and Nationalism: Theory and Comparison,* New Delhi: Sage Publications, 1991.

Brass, Paul R., *Religion, Language and Politics in North India,* Cambridge: Cambridge University Press, 1974.

Broom, David, "Ethnicity, Nationalism and Democracy in South East Asia," in *Ethnicity* (ed.) John Hutchinson and Anthony D. Smith; New York: Oxford University Press, 1996.

Burgess, M.E., "The Resource of Enthnicity: Myth or Reality", *Ethnic and Racial Studies,* 1:3 (July 1973).

Campbell, Agnus, "Surge and Decline: A Study of Electoral Change," *Public Opinion Quarterly,* 24, 1960.

Cross, M., "Colonialism and Ethnicity: A Theory and Comparative Case Study, *Ethnic and Racial Studies.* 1:1 (Jan. 1975).

Connor, W., "The Politics of the Enthno-Nationalism", *Journal of International Affairs,* 27:1 (1975).

Connor, W., "A Nation is a Nation, is a State, is an Ethnic Group, is a ....." *Ethnic and Racial Studies,* 1:4 (1978).

Connor, W., "Beyond Reason: The Nature of the Ethnonational Bond," in *Ethnicity* (ed.) John Hutchinson and Anthony, D. Smith, New York: Oxford University Press, 1996.

Connor, W., "Nation Building or Nation Destroying?" *World Politics* 24:3 (April, 1972).

Coleman, James, *Nigeria: Background to Nationalism,* Berkely: University of Chicago, 1958.

Curtis, Gerald, *Election Campaigning Japanese Style,* New York: Colombia University Press, 1971.

David, James, *Human Nature in Politics,* New York: Wiley, 1963.

Deutsch, Karl W., *Nationalism and Social Communication,* Cambridge: MIT Press, 1966.

Deutsch, Karl W. and Foltz, William J. (eds.), *National Building,* New York: Atherton, 1973.

Deutsch, Karl W., "Social Mobilization and Political Development," *American Political Science Review* (September, 1961).

Dube, S.C., *Modernization and Development: The Search for Alternative Paradigm,* New Delhi: Vistaar Publication, 1988.

Elder, Joseph W., National Loyalties in a Newly Independent Nation, in *Ideology and Discontent,* (ed.) David Apter, London: The Free Press of Glencoe, 1964.

Embree, Ainglie T., "Pluralism and National Integration: The Indian Experience," *Journal of International Affairs,* 27:1 (1973).

Emerson, R., *From Empire to Nation,* Cambridge: Massachusetts, 1960.

Enloe, C.H., *Ethnic Conflict and Political Development,* Boston: Little Brown and Company, 1973.

Enloe, C.H., "Internal Colonialism, Federalism and Alternative State Development Strategies," *Publics,* 7:4 (1977).

Enloe, C.H., "Central Government's Strategies for Coping with Separatist Movement", in *The Politics of Separation* (ed.) W.H. Morris Jones, London: University of London Institute of Common Wealth Studies Collected Seminar Papers, 1976.

Esmen, M.J. (ed.), *Ethnic Conflict in the Western World,* New York: Cornell University Press, 1977.

Eisenstadt, S.N. and Rokkan, S. (eds.) *Building States and Nation,* 2 Vols., Beverly Hills: Sage Publications, 1973.

Foon, C.S., "On the Incompatibility of Ethnic and National Loyalties: Reframing the Issues, "*Canadian Review of Studies in Nationalism,* 3:1 (1986).

Gans, Herbert J., "Symbolic Ethnicity", in *Ethnicity* (ed.) John Hutchinson and Anthony D. Smith, New York: Oxford University Press, 1996.

Gans, H., "Symbolic Ethnicity: The Future of Ethnic Groups and Cultures in America", *Ethnic and Racial Studies* 2:1 (1979).

George and Ross (eds.), *Ethnic Identity: Cultural Continuities and Change,* California: May Field Publishing Company, 1975.

Glazer, Nathan and Moynihan, Daniel Patrick, *Beyond the Melting Pot,* Massachusetts: The MIT Press, 1963.

Greeley, *Ethnicity in the United States: A Preliminary Reconnaissance,* New York: Wiley, 1974.

Greetz, Clifford M. (ed.), *Societies and New States,* New York: Free Press, 1963.

Grove, D.J., "A Test of the Ethnic Equalization Hypothesis: A Cross National Study", *Ethnic and Racial Studies,* 1:2 (1978).

Hardgrave, R.L., *The Dravidian Movement,* Bombay: Popular Prakashan, 1965.

Hayes, Carleton, *The Historical Evolution of Modern Nationalism,* New York: Richard R. Smith, 1931.

Hecter, Michael and Levi, Margarett, "The Comparative Analysis of Ethno-regional Movements," *Ethnic and Racial Studies,* 2:3 (July, 1979).

Heisler, Martion O., "Ethnic Conflict in the World Today", *The Annals of American Academy of Political and Social Sciences,* 433, 1977.

Hodgkin, Thomas, *Nationalism and Colonial Africa,* New York: Atherton, 1957.

Horowitz, Donald L., "Patterns of Ethnic Separatism", *Comparative Studies in Society and History,* 23:2 (April, 1981).

Horowitz, D.L., *Ethnic Groups in Conflict,* Los Angeles, University of California Press, 1985.

Hutchinson, John and Smith, A.D., *Ethnicity,* New York: Oxford University Press, 1996.

Irschick, E.F., *Tamil Rvivalism in 1930s,* Chennai: Cre-A Publications, 1986.

Jacob, Phillip E. and Toscano, James V. (eds.), *The Integration of Political Communities,* Philadelphia: Wily, 1964.

Karunanidhi, M., *Kalaignar Kaditham,* Vols. I-X, Chennai: Abirami Nilayam, 1986.

Kavanagh, Dennis, *Political Culture,* London: MacMillan, 1972.

Kim, Jae-on, Nie, Norman H. and Verba, Sidney, "The Amount and Concentration of Political Activity," *Political Methodology* 1:2 (1974).

Kohn, Hans, *The Idea of Nationalism,* New York: Wiley, 1961.

Kothari, Rajini, "Integration and Performance: Two Pivots of India's Model of Nation Building," in *State and Nation Building : A*

Third World Perspective (ed.) Rajni Kothari, New Delhi: Allied Publishers Private Limited, 1976.

Lerner, Daniel, *The Passing of Traditional Society,* Glencoe: Illinois, 1995.

Lightbody, James, "A Note on the Theory of Nationalism as a Function of Ethnic Demands," *Canadian Journal of Political Science,* 2:3 (1969).

Lipset, S.M., *The First New Nation,* New York: Wiley, 1963.

Lustick, I., "Deeply Divided Societies: Consociationalism *versus* Control," *World Politics,* 31:325-344, 1979.

Mckinsey, L.S., "Dimensions for National Political Integration and Disintegration: The Case of Quebec Separatism 1960-75," *Comparative Political Studies,* 9:3 (1976).

MIDS, *Tamil Nadu Economy:Performence and Issues,* New Delhi: Oxford & IBH Publishing Co. Pvt. Ltd., 1988.

Milbrath, Laster, W., *Political Participation,* Chicago: Rand Mc Nally & Company, 1965.

Morris-Jones W.H. (ed.), *The Politics of Separation,* London: University of London, 1976.

Nagata, Judith, "The Status of Ethnicity and the Ethnicity of Status," *International Journal of Comparative Sociology,* 17:2, 1976.

Oomman, T.K., *Citizenship and National Identity: From Colonialism to Globalization,* New Delhi: Sage Publications, 1977.

Palanithurai, G., "Ethnic Leader and Social Change: A Study in Micro Modelling," *Journal of Annamalai University,* Part A 33, 1989.

Palanithurai, G., *Management of Ethnic Conflict in India and Canada,* New Delhi: Kanishka Publishers and Distributors, 1995.

Palanithurai G., *People's Perception of Politics: An Indian Perspective,* New Delhi: Kanishka Publishers and Distributors, 1995.

Palanithurai, G., *Political Communications and Political Mobilization: A Study in Dravidian Movement,* Annamalai Nagar: Department of Political Science, 1989.

Palaniturai, G., "Indian Politics from the Perspective of Tamil Nadu Polity," *The The Indian Journal of Public Affairs and Policy Research,* 1 & 2: 1-4 (Jan.-Dec., 2000).

Palanithurai, G., *Ethnic Movement in India: Theory and Practice.* New Delhi: Kanishka Publishers and Distributors, 1993.

Palanithurai, G. and Thandavan, R. (ed.), *Perspective on Indian Regionalism;* New Delhi: Kanishka Publishers and Distributors, 1993.

Pandian, M.S.S., *M.G. Ramachandran in Film and Politics : The Image Trap,* New Delhi : Sage Publications, 1992.

Preez, P.D., *The Politics of Identity Ideology and the Human Image,* Oxford: Basil Blackwell, 1980.

Rajagopal, Indhu, *The Tyranny of Caste: The Non-Brahmin Movement and Political Development in South India,* New Delhi: Vikas Publishing House, 1985.

Riggs, Fred W., Ethnicity, *International Conceptual Encyclopaedia for the Social Sciences,* Vol. I, New York: UNESCO, 1985.

Royce, A.P., *Ethnic Identity : Strategies of Diversity,* Bloomington: Indiana University Press, 1982.

Remcikis, Thomas, "Modernization and National Identity in the Baltic Republics: Uneven and Multi-dimensional Change in the Componenets of Modernization," in *Nationalism and Human Rights: Process of Modernization in the USSR* (ed.) Ihor Kamenesky, Littleton: Lievaries Unlimited Inc, 1977.

Rothschild, Joseph, *Ethnopolitics: A Conceptual Framework,* New York: Columbia University Press, 1981.

Sagarin, E. and Moneymaker, James, "Language and Nationalist Separatist Movements," in *Ethnic Autonomy: Comparative Dynamics* (ed.) R. Hall, New York: Pergamon Press, 1979.

Sears, David D., "Political Socialization," in *Handbook of Political Science:Micro Political Theory* (ed.) Greenstein and Polsby, Sidney: Addison Wesley Publishing Company, 1975.

Shanmugam, S.V., *Mozhi Valarchiyum Mozhi Unarvum (Tamil),* Madras: Manivasakar Padhippagam, 1989.

Sivathambi, K., *Understanding Dravidian Movement,* Madras: New Century Book House, 1986.

Smith, A.D., "The Myth of the Modern Nation and the Myth of Nations," *Ethnic and Racial Studies,* 3,1: 1-25, 1988.

Smith, A.D., *State and Nation in the Third World,* Brighton: Harvester Press, 1983.

Smith, A,D., *Nations and Nationalism in a Global Era,* Cambridge: Polity Press, 1995.

Smith, A.D., *The Ethnic Origin of Nations,* Oxford: Blackwell, 1986.

Smith, A.D., *National Identity,* Harmonds Worth: Penguine, 1991.

Smith, A.D., *The Ethnic Origin of Nations,* Oxford: Basil Blackwell, 1986.

Schubert, James, N., Wiegele, Thomas C. and Hines, Samuel M., Jr., *Age, Age Related Structure and Political Decision-Making [A Final Report to the National Institute of Aging],* J. Dckalf Northern llionis University, 1986.

Subramaniam, Narendra, *Ethnicity and Populist Mobilization,* New Delhi: Oxford University Press, 1999.

Tagil, Steven (ed.), *Ethnicity and Nation Building in the Nardic World,* London: Horst and Company, 1995.

Thompson, D.L. and Ronen, Dov, (eds.) *Ethnicity. Politics and Development,* Colorado : Lynne Rienner Publishers, 1986.

Veeramani, K., *Periyar and Women's Rights,* Chennai: Emerald Publishers,1994.

Verba, Sidney, Nie, Norman H. and Kim, Jae-on, *Participation and Political Equality: A Seven Nation Comparison,* Cambridge: Cambridge University Press, 1978.

Verba, Sidney, Nie, Norman H. and Kim, Jae-on, *The Modes of Democratic Participation : A Cross National Analysis,* California: Sage Professional Papers in Comparative Politics, 1971.

Verba, Sidney, Nie, Norman H., Barbic Ana, Irwin, Galen, Molleman, Henk and Shabad Goldie, "The Seven Modes of Participation : Continuities in Reséarch," *Comparative Political Studies* 6:235-250, 1973.

Verba, Sidney, Nie, Norman H., *Participation in America: Political Democracy and Social Equality,* New York: Harper & Row Publishers, 1972.

Vincent, Joan, "The Structuring of Ethnicity," *Human Organization,* 23:4 376-377 (1974).

Vos, George De, "Ethnic Pluralism," in *Enthnic Identity: Cultural Continuities and Change* (ed.) George De Vos, Ross and Lola Romanucci, California : May Field Publishing Company, 1975.

Worseley, P., *The Three Worlds : Culture and Worlds Developments,* Chicago: Chicago University Press, 1984.

Watson, Seton H., *Nations and States,* London : Methuen, 1977.

Yinger, J.M., "Towards a Theory of Assimilation and Dissimulation," *Ethnic and Racial Studies,* 4:3 (1981).

Yinger, J.M., "Ethnicity in Complex Societies: Structural, Cultural and Charactrological Factors," in *The Uses of Controversy in Sociology,* (ed.) L. Coses and O. Larson, New York: Free Press, 1976.

Young, Crawford, *The Politics of Cultural Pluralism,* Madison : The University of Wisconsin Press, 1976.

INDEX